The
Province
of
Sociology

The Province of Sociology

Selected Profiles

William A. Pearman
and Robert Rotz

Nelson-Hall nh Chicago

Library of Congress Cataloging in Publication Data

Pearman, William A   1940-
   The province of sociology.

   Bibliography: p.
   Includes index.
   1. Sociology—History. 2. Sociologists—Biography. I. Rotz, Robert,
1926-   joint author. II. Title.
HM19.P35   301'.092'2   79-17996
ISBN 0-88229-434-2 (Cloth)
ISBN 0-88229-735-X (Paper)

Manufactured in the United States of America

10   9   8   7   6   5   4   3   2   1

Contents

Introduction 1

1. At the Beginning 7

   Auguste Comte 8
   Charles Darwin 12
   Emile Durkheim 14
   Thomas R. Malthus 19
   Karl Marx 22
   Vilfredo Pareto 26
   Georg Simmel 29
   Herbert Spencer 32
   Gabriel Tarde 34
   Ferdinand Toennies 36
   Lester F. Ward 39
   Max Weber 41

2. The Beginnings in America 49

   Charles Horton Cooley 50
   Franklin H. Giddings 53
   George Herbert Mead 56
   Robert E. Park 59
   Albion Small 61
   William Graham Sumner 64
   William I. Thomas 67

3. Sharpening the Focus 71

Reinhard Bendix 73
Ernest W. Burgess 75
F. Stuart Chapin 77
Kingsley Davis 79
William J. Goode 82
August B. Hollingshead 84
Everett C. Hughes 85
George A. Lundberg 87
Helen & Robert S. Lynd 88
Karl Mannheim 90
C. Wright Mills 93
William F. Ogburn 95
Pitirim Sorokin 98
Edwin H. Sutherland 101
William Lloyd Warner 103
William F. Whyte 105
Louis Wirth 106
Florian Znaniecki 108

4. Enhancing the Focus 111

Gordon W. Allport 111
Ruth Benedict 113
John Dewey 116
Sigmund Freud 119
Erich Fromm 124
Kurt Lewin 127
Bronislaw Malinowski 129
Margaret Mead 132
Robert Michels 134
George P. Murdock 135

Gunnar Myrdal 135
Robert Redfield 138
Thomas S. Szasz 141
Thorstein Veblen 142

5. Contemporary Contributors 145

Howard S. Becker 146
Daniel Bell 147
Peter Berger 150
Peter M. Blau 151
James S. Coleman 153
Lewis A. Coser 154
Donald G. Cressey 155
Ralf Dahrendorf 157
Amitai W. Etzioni 159
Herbert Gans 162
Erving Goffman 163
Alvin W. Gouldner 164
George C. Homans 166
Mirra Komarovsky 168
Paul F. Lazarsfeld 170
Seymour M. Lipset 171
Robert Merton 174
Robert A. Nisbet 177
Talcott Parsons 179
David Riesman 183
Robin M. Williams 186

Bibliography 189

Index 201

Introduction

There is no study more important, nor any pursuit more critical in our time, than that which has come to be called sociology. Our very survival may depend on the products of this study of man in society.

Although its history as a science is less than two centuries old, the impulses eventuating in the study of society are quite ancient. Man has long sought to understand his own essential nature and that of the social order which he unconsciously or purposively fashioned. Much of this effort, expended over thousands of years, is probably attributable to man's marked curiosity, often considered a basic trait of the human being, but it is questionable whether this motivation alone suffices as an explanation. A more plausible view is that the various manifestations of early social organization necessitated further adjustments. That is, when man no longer had to follow the food supply, when agriculture was discovered, he could live together in larger groups and thus enhance his culture. With the resultant organization, man became heir to conditions that were perceived as undesirable or potentially destructive. Therefore, there were practical reasons for seeking knowledge relative to the social order—problem solving!

The history of man is replete with illustrations of insensitivity, injustice, brutality, suffering, and death. When man reached the point in his development wherein he would pose the question Why must this be? he was initiating a line of inquiry pursued by Auguste Comte in the nineteenth century. Comte, a student at the prestigious Ecole Polytechnique, founder of modern sociology, would ask, in effect, How can human progress be achieved consistent with order? Why is the social order not more perfect? How can we improve society? Comte was disturbed by the chaotic effects of the French Revolution to the extent that he called

1

for a science of society, which he felt was necessary for social improvement. We still seek the answers to these and a host of related questions, but we do so with increasing urgency, fearing that our problems are already beyond our control.

Mankind has survived plague, pestilence, disease, starvation, war, and degradation, which evidences, if nothing else, his resilience, persistence, and will. His present state, though, is precarious at best and perhaps more treacherous than when, during the early stages of his development, he was struggling to achieve dominance over threatening aspects of the environment. John F. Kennedy once said, "We happen to live in the most dangerous time in the history of the human race."

In modern times we have experienced such ultimate obscenities and barbarities as Dachau, Belsen, and Buchenwald. Further, we must now adjust to the fact that with our sophisticated technological capacity entire populations can be annihilated many times over. Chemical and biological warfare remain as threats; and recent recombinant DNA research—"genetic engineering"—has caused concern that new life forms could devastate animal and plant life. It would appear that we can, in fact, create the predicted situation in which the living, if any, envy the dead.

Unfortunately, though man has been remarkably brilliant in terms of technological expertise, he has been eminently dull-witted in attempts to match such achievements with social inventions. Early man possessed crude techniques for solving technical and human problems. Adjustments for the latter included adoption, enslavement, and killing. Modern man, utilizing the same basic adjustments or their variants (as he has in this century), could conceivably return humankind to the level of the primitive on all counts. There is hope that wisdom will preclude that possibility. However, one need not be a confirmed cynic or pessimist to note that to date man's record for employing humane solutions is not encouraging.

The preceding posture of gloom is not a philippic against modernity or the obvious advantages of technology. It merely points up the critical need to gain accurate insights into the nature of man and society and thereby greater dominion over ourselves. In this quest, sociology can be of great value.

Sociology represents no formal messianic mission. It presents no panacea for the world's ills, no magic formulae for fashioning utopias. However, that is not to imply that sociologists are concerned simply with observing what is; many are engaged in promoting change, directly or indirectly. Candor demands the admission that sociology, like other branches of knowledge, is not value-free. Though many, in the interest of achieving greater scientific respectability, would deny it, their interest in knowing transcends the satisfaction of knowing. The discipline was born in an atmosphere of philosophic and reformist tendencies. The sociologist is now scientific insofar as he employs scientific methodology; he does not reside in a value vacuum. In truth, though he functions by the canons of scientific research, he also (if we can avoid semantic nuances) manifests faith—faith that through science, the most reliable source of truth, man's lot can be improved or his potential enchanced. Thus, in systematically studying society, in either micro- or macrocosm, the sociologist is not engaged in some intellectual ritual; he is approaching the most dramatic frontier in human experience—a comprehensive understanding of human nature and human society in the usually unstated interest of prediction and a consequent adjustment between man and his environment.

Like love, sociology is not easily defined. The term that Comte used to replace "positive philosophy" refers roughly to the study of society on a high level of abstraction. It implies also a generic approach to social phenomena; in fact, some look upon sociology as a science that synthesizes knowledge from other disciplines. Most would agree that sociology is the rigorous, scientific, and thus relatively objective study of human interaction. The sociologist is primarily interested in discovering the social bases of human group behavior. In that effort he deals with factors such as: biological influences on behavior, the individual personality, group processes, social systems or institutions, the impact of culture on behavior, and combinations and permutations of numerous variables as they contribute to the social order. The specific concern of the sociologist is the interaction that occurs within and between these factors and the resultant patterning of behavior.

The study of human group behavior and of the nature of society in general is a complex and multifaceted endeavor. The study of man as a social animal falls squarely within the province of sociology as the boundaries of the discipline are customarily drawn. Classificatory systems are usually imposed arbitrarily on nature, but human knowledge, like other natural phenomena, cannot be so neatly and rigidly categorized. A rich and impressive list of social perspectives, theories, and concepts has arisen from the efforts that political scientists, historians, anthropologists, philosophers, economists, psychiatrists, and others have expended to understand selected aspects of the social order. Concerted interdisciplinary efforts and the proliferation of subfields in these and other disciplines have created an extensive body of knowledge relative to social reality.

It is the view of the authors that the boundaries of sociology are not fixed and rigidly defined.

Most, if not all, generalizations about the nature of social structures and functions are, we believe, within the realm of sociological interest. Therefore, some individuals who are not technically sociologists are nevertheless recognized in this work as major contributors to the field.

Considering the fact that sociology is a generic science, linked with some evidence that it has a tendency toward intellectual imperialism, the dimensions of the province are apt to be overwhelming to the layman, staggering to the student, and challenging to the professional. The professional may eventually find it difficult to maintain an overall perspective on the field, inasmuch as he usually becomes a specialist in one of its many subfields. Since no scientist becomes an expert on things in general, the price of expertise is narrow specialization.

With the preceding in mind, we have attempted to produce a book that will serve the needs and interests of the individuals with widely divergent backgrounds. We hope that professionals in various disciplines will find the work useful as an abbreviated review. It is written also for the initiate in sociology or, indeed, in some other social science, who wants more than a passing acquaintance with some of the leading figures associated with social theory.

The general purpose of this book is to introduce some of the major contributors in the realm of sociology, along with the salient theories and concepts attributed to them. It is not a work on theory per se. Rather it is intended as a convenient, theory-related, intellectual tool-guide that will point up the critical importance of social research and theory and render the latter more accessible. Our specific objectives are:

a. to acquaint the reader with a broad sampling of contributors to the study of human interaction and the social order;

b. to review the basis for the prominence of selected leading figures;

c. to enhance the reader's interest and comprehension with interpretive pen and ink illustrations that will fix in the mind an image of some of the contributors;

d. to present theories and concepts not as isolated, remote ideas, but as serious mental products of flesh and blood human beings;

e. to extend the personal parameters of sociological theory; and

f. to produce a reference for all, novice and expert alike, who are interested (or may become interested) in the study of social interaction.

Toward these ends the authors have included in the profiles (with certain exceptions) a variety of information: personal data on the subjects, intellectual influences on them, their association with subfields, their theoretical impact, and an analysis of major concepts in their works. The general movement of the book is chronological. The individuals within each section are introduced alphabetically.

As with any work of this type, difficult and ultimately arbitrary decisions had to be made concerning inclusions and exclusions. An extensive list of important contemporaries comes easily to mind. We deeply regret all exclusions, especially since we have unbounded respect and appreciation for all who have contributed in any way to the sociological view of reality.

Chapter 1

At the Beginning

One cannot appreciate the current state of a discipline without understanding its origins. This is also one way of defining a field or deciding what lies within its province.

In this initial section we discuss those individuals who are identified with the early state of sociology as a discipline. The capsule descriptions contained here should give the reader a feeling for the eclectic origins of sociology and for subsequent developments in its perspective. Although a number of the men discussed were not sociologists as such, their work and ideas form the foundations of the discipline and enlarge its parameters. The diverse backgrounds they represent have in part been responsible for the multifaceted development of sociology.

The twelve theorists included in this section—Comte, Darwin, Durkheim, Malthus, Marx, Pareto, Simmel, Spencer, Tarde, Toennies, Ward and Weber—exhibit intellectual as well as geographic diversity. Some, like Comte, Spencer, and Pareto, attempted to define sociology. Malthus and Darwin, both Englishmen, worked in other fields, probably not at all interested in the nature of sociology, but their contributions in their own fields had important consequences for future directions of sociological inquiry.

Darwin's contribution to models of evolutionary thought set a tone for early inquiry. Spencer and others discussed here can be regarded as being in the Darwinian tradition. Thomas Malthus, one of the thinkers admired by Darwin, alerted social thinkers to the need for inquiry into population, which he recognized as an important societal variable.

Some of the men held rather narrow definitions of sociology, its nature, and appropriate methodology. Tarde's focus on the process of imitation and Marx's concern for the unequal distribution of the means of production are examples of narrow social interpretations. Others, such as Weber, Simmel, and Durkheim, developed much broader perspectives and examined a wide spectrum of societal variables. In Pareto we find an early theorist who, trained in the natural sciences but later interested in economics, began to develop a framework for a broad systemization of social science.

The men discussed here made many significant contributions and, like the other writers treated in this volume, all labored for objective scientific inquiry.

It is best to point out that upon finishing this opening section, the reader will have a far greater feel for the diversity of sociology than for its coherence.

AUGUSTE COMTE

Auguste Comte, the father of sociology, was born in Montpellier, France, in 1798. He was born into a Catholic family of royalist background, his father having been a civil servant of reasonable means. Comte, however, rebelled against this background and upon entering the Ecole Polytechnique became involved in the republican cause in politics. This affiliation caused him to be expelled as a subversive. Perhaps the most profound influence on Comte's development was his intellectual association with Claude Henri de Rouvroy, comte de Saint-Simon, to whom he served as a private secretary from 1817 to 1823.

It is interesting that an intellectual as adept at philosophy, mathematics, and then sociology as Comte was never held a university teaching post. He survived mainly on income from public lectures in Paris, school examiner's fees, and from the good will of his friends, John Stuart Mill and George Grote. In 1830 he founded the Association Polytechnique, a group dedicated to the education of working-class youths.

The later years of his life were spent in the development of a godless religion, one that retained the institutional trappings of the

AUGUSTE COMTE

9

Catholicism he had repudiated as a youth. In this endeavor he founded the Société positiviste, devoted to the promulgation of the "cult of humanity."

Although broad in scope, Comte's writing was unified by his concern with the problem of knowledge: its nature, its structure, and its acquisition. Under the previous psychologistic approach, knowledge was treated as a function of certain mental states. Positivism, a methodological and epistemological doctrine, maintained that knowledge could be understood only by examining its growth and historical dimensions. Comte stressed that the collective history of thought rather than the individual psyche was the force that illuminated the conditions and limits of human knowledge. He was intrigued not by the state of knowledge, but by its progressive development. This interest followed from the influence of Condorcet and Saint-Simon.

Comte's most significant formulation concerning the development of thought can be found in his "law of the three states." He postulated that human thought in its historical development passes successively through three phases: the theological, the metaphysical, and the positive. He compared these to fictional, abstract, and scientific stages. The positive state repudiated both the causal forces of the metaphysical and the divine forces of the theological state, restricting itself to verifiable correlations between observable phenomena. He viewed the development of knowledge as an evolutionary process, with the theological and metaphysical states as necessary forerunners of the positive.

In his *Cours de philosophie positive* Comte attempted to assess movement toward the positive state in various individual sciences. The result was his hierarchy of sciences, in which he ranked them as follows according to how closely they approached the positive state: mathematics, astronomy, physics, chemistry, biology, and sociology, then termed social physics. Only mathematics and astronomy, he asserted, had actually reached the positive state.

Comte's hierarchy referred to additional characteristics of knowledge, excluding mathematics. It represented methodological characteristics and increasing complexity in subject matter. He maintained that astronomy was based on observation, biology on observation and experimentation, sociology on a unique historical method. Comte's purpose in this exercise was to seek out the unity in science.

The balancing of mental inquisitiveness and empirical controls in the creation of knowledge was one of Comte's contributions to scientific method. He argued against the empiricists in that he saw the need for imagination in a researcher's attempt to generate a hypothesis; yet verification is central to his stages of knowledge, distinguishing the metaphysical from the positive. Theories need not have been generated in experimentation, but they had to be subjected to experimental verification in order to be establishd as scientific. Comte criticized those physical theories of his day as well as earlier beliefs which he felt were unverifiable and representative of the bygone metaphysical epoch. He established the doctrine of verifiability as central to both science and philosophy. He also advocated prediction as a proper function of the scientist. His belief that the ideal science, given empirically determined initial conditions, can deduce subsequent system states is modeled after the theories of Laplace and Lagrange.

Although he was primarily a natural scientist, Comte's writings on social physics are of most interest here. He characterized most writing about man's social nature as speculative rather than empirical and contended that theological and metaphysical perspectives were blocks to objective study. Social dynamics—the origins, growth, and development through a life cycle by society and social groupings—became the subject of Comte's new science.

He linked society to the biological and physiological characteristics of its members but also emphasized historical elements, for history was central to his conception of sociology. The institutions and structure of any society were, he argued, determined by its previous conditions.

He contended that the sociologist, whom he charged with studying the evolution of human institutions, could understand society and predict its course only if he knew the past. The sociologist uses history to study this past, but it makes sense to him only in terms of known laws of human nature, either biological or psychological. Through his historical method Comte is thus concerned with the unity and interdependence of science.

The basic concept of sociological analysis for Comte was progress. He meant intellectual progress of course, and he attributed social change not to political or economic forces, but to intellectual ones. The sociology of knowledge was, in his view, the basis of sociology.

It is indeed unfortunate that Comte's influence on modern sociology is underplayed. Too often he is dismissed merely as the person who coined the name for the field. His argument for extending the methods of physical science to sociology is meaningful in retrospect, for followers such as John Stuart Mill and Claude Bernard were important figures in the development of science. Although it was initially looked upon with disfavor, Comtean positivism was an important force in a later philosophical critique of the sciences by such thinkers as Ernst Mach and Pierre Duhem. Logical positivists in the twentieth century also uphold certain Comtean ideals.

CHARLES DARWIN

Charles Darwin was the most influential proponent of evolutionary theory that science has ever known. His major work, *Origin of Species,* was written in 1859 and was the result of world travels during which he classified thousands of life forms and fossil traces thereof. His major thesis was that the human race had evolved gradually from lower orders of life as a progressive adaptation to the environment through the survival of those forms best adapted to a competitive struggle.

Seizing upon the biological thesis offered by Darwin, early sociologists tried to discern an evolutionary pattern in the development of human culture and social life. Comte, for example, had seen such patterns in human thought, and Spencer was highly enthusiastic in his descriptions of societal evolution. Both Comte and Spencer saw society as evolving toward increased human happiness.

Darwin's influence is evident in Spencer's terminology: His writings discuss "survival of the fittest" and refer to the victories of one group of people over another as the conquest of the more adapted over the less adapted.

CHARLES DARWIN

13

Darwin, who also wrote *The Descent of Man* (1871), did not discuss questions of social philosophy in his writing. In fact, when contrasting social and biological processes of evolution he emphasized the latter. This mattered little to those nineteenth-century sociologists who believed that Darwin's theory of biological evolution provided a model for the study of society. They generally substituted social groups for biological organisms in their transference of the theory to society. Counted as Social Darwinists are men such as Walter Bagehot, Ludwig Gumplowicz, Gustav Ratzenhofer, and William Graham Sumner. Their overall theoretical orientation has virtually disappeared from the sociological mainstream, but a number of by-products remain, such as insights into social conflict.

EMILE DURKHEIM

Emile Durkheim was born in Epinal, France, in 1858. He emerged as an important early figure in sociology through his substantive studies in the areas of religion, suicide, and the division of labor in society. The bulk of his work was devoted to the concept of social organization. His explication of the constructs of societal integration and regulation furthered the development of sociology. Durkheim also contributed to the methodology of empirical social research, although later scholars questioned the validity of his usage of empirical and ecological data.

Durkheim helped achieve an identity for the emerging field of sociology by recommending it as both a mechanism for the development of society and a remedy for social problems. He viewed institutions such as education and religion as potential instruments for social reform.

Durkheim subscribed to the point of view that society represents a reality greater than the sum total of its individual parts. Society, he said, is the outcome of human group interaction and organization; hence, it is inexplicable in terms of the characteristics of individual members. He reasoned that society is "real" because (1) the structure of social organization leads to phenomena that individuals do not experience and (2) individuals undergo change as a result of participation in society. There is some controversy as to whether or not Durkheim advocated group mind as an ex-

EMILE DURKHEIM

15

planatory concept. In his early writing he claimed that individuals alone are conscious, or have minds, but he later placed increased emphasis on a group consciousness. Individuals, he said, are the creation of group life; society precedes and creates the individual. To understand the individual, we must first understand the social.

Of particular concern to Durkheim was the question of social integration and how order is achieved in society. His answer to this puzzle appears in his discussion of the forces of solidarity. He proposed two types: mechanical and organic solidarity.

Mechanical solidarity he equated with the solidarity of sameness. Societies bound by mechanical solidarity are less complex societies characterized by low division of labor. The many shared experiences of the participants create a leveling force which Durkheim referred to as the "collective conscience." In *The Division of Labor in Society,* he explained that simplistic societies are integrated through this collective conscience, which prescribes the details of daily life. In such societies rational choice is not a factor; violation of the social order or pursuit of individual gain are not realistic options.

Complex, technologically advanced societies are held together by a solidarity of differences. This Durkheim called organic solidarity. Here he approximated the thinking of Herbert Spencer, using biological organisms as analogies in constructing his schema. Separation of functions, or high division of labor, creates interdependence among societal parts. According to Durkheim, the specialization that results from the separation of societal functions and institutions leads to a solidarity based upon reciprocal needs. This thinking serves as a base for the sociological study of elites. A set of general rules paralleling the collective conscience of the less complex societies governs the relationships among the individual societal parts. How these rules arise is unclear, but they embrace general social values such as justice and honesty. These traits supposedly promote social order by insuring that individuals enter into relations which are in the societal interest. In both mechanically and organically oriented societies Durkheim saw social order developing from social constraint rather than individual will.

In *The Elementary Forms of Religious Life,* Durkheim modified the above position, suggesting that social constraint came into being through the personalities of societal members. They internalize society's rules and seek conformity to moral principles that symbolize the needs of society, which they have also internalized. Negative sanctions in the form of punishment reaffirm society's standards and induce individuals to respect its moral codes.

The methodological interests expressed in *Rules of the Sociological Method* illustrate Durkheim's concern with social realism. Here he argues that social facts are as real as physical facts. A social fact is external to the individual and constraining of him. Durkheim observed that people behave toward the social world and its facts (such as institutional spheres and their functionaries) as they do toward physical facts.

The acceptance of the reality of social facts, Durkheim argued, is basic to the development of sociology as a science. The objects of sociological study must be conceived of as independent of the investigator's will. In his study of social phenomena, the sociologist must search not inside but outside the actor for an explanation of his behavior. Such study requires a specialized method, Durkheim advised. One can study social facts only through the use of objective indicators, which allow measurement of phenomena not directly observable. The use of social indicators has become a prominent feature of late twentieth-century sociological methodology.

Durkheim's theories on internalization of norms by members of society are important to the sociological perspective. The process of socialization, the learning of societal norms and expectations, is of central interest in modern sociology. The continuity of societal expectations around social behavior lends creditability to the social realism of Durkheim. In emphasizing agreement on basic social values, his analysis of society provided a springboard for theorists who operate in the sociological tradition now labeled as structural functionalism. The wisdom of his observations on organic solidarity, in which interdependence becomes the binding force, is apparent as society becomes more urban and complex.

His contributions to the subfield of sociology of religion are also valuable. He urged sociologists to know a society and its culture before attempting to identify what its members regard as sacred. Because those objects treated as sacred vary throughout the world, the sociologist wishing to understand the symbols of a group must first study the group in depth in order to understand the referents for the symbols.

Society, as Durkheim saw it, was the object of religious worship. Religion, in whatever form, supports society by reinforcing the system of social control. It makes adherence to society's values and rules a sacred obligation. Durkheim compared man's relation to society and its social order to that of the believer before his God. Just as people feel an inner peace when they believe themselves to be in harmony with the supernatural, they feel good when they are in harmony with the social order that surrounds them.

Durkheim's study of suicide has become a classic study of the relationship between the societal and individual levels of organization. Unfortunately, students often concern themselves with the descriptive content of his typology, forgetting his intention to study suicide within the context of social organization. He described three ideal types of suicide based on degree of societal integration, as reflected in an individual's commitment to the normative structure of society and its institutions.

The first type, altruistic suicide, occurs when societal integration is so complete that society can demand that the individual take his life for it. Suicide can also occur in opposite situations; i.e., when individuals do not possess strong societal or group ties. This Durkheim referred to as egoistic suicide. Anomic suicides are traceable to confusion about societal norms or to rapid change in societal institutions, both of which can cause individuals to apply incorrect social rules in given situations.

Recent theorists argue that there is no distinction in Durkheim's work between egoism and anomie, or between the causes of these two types of suicide. The French term *anomie* has since been widely used in the study of social problems related to social disorganization. Merton, for example, develops this point in his work, *Social Theory and Social Structure.*

Used as an underpinning in the study of other forms of deviance, particularly juvenile delinquency, Durkheim's description of egoistic suicide inspired the constraint theory of deviance. In his observation of suicide rates, Durkheim noted a higher incidence of suicide among Protestants as opposed to Catholics and Jews, among single as opposed to married individuals and among childless couples as opposed to parents. He viewed Catholics and Jews, married people, and couples with children as being more integrated into their respective social groups. Persons without group ties he felt were more prone to commit deviant acts such as suicide because life was less meaningful to them. Studies of alienation in modern society will find theoretical supports in the work of Durkheim. So much of his work, despite methodological problems, is relevant in the late twentieth century.

THOMAS R. MALTHUS

Thomas Malthus (1766-1834) was an English clergyman who believed that biological principles could be used to solve social problems. Although he was not a sociologist, Malthus provided valuable insights into the study of population, an important subfield within the discipline. His theory was instrumental in the development of Darwinism, which had a direct impact on the early directions of sociology.

Malthus was a disciple of Adam Smith, the famous economist who embodied the laissez-faire thesis in his landmark book, *The Wealth of Nations.* Whereas Smith was optimistic about the future of society and the possibilities of social reform, Malthus was pessimistic about it. He witnessed the rapid industrialization of Europe, particularly England, and focused on the trend's concomitant social evils. Malthus's ideas were not readily accepted in his lifetime, for they were regarded as too negative. In America his theories were attacked by the classical political economist Henry C. Carey, who defended the optimism expressed by Adam Smith.

Malthus is now recognized as the first major student of population. Being concerned with the consequences of unrestricted population growth, he posited that population tends to increase geometrically, while the food supply increases arithmetically. Utilizing available data on London and other major urban centers, he observed that population growth increased annually,

Thomas R. Malthus

20

while the food supply remained relatively stable. He was firm in his prediction that the discrepancy between food supply and population would become greater with each passing year, and he feared that population would soon outstrip available food supplies. He talked of both positive and preventive checks on population growth. As examples of positive checks he cited famine, death, and disease, while preventive checks included voluntary birth control, infanticide, and killing of the aged, sick, or infirm.

Malthus had expected that population would double each quarter of a century. His dire predictions did not materialize for a number of reasons: improvements in agriculture, the discovery of new lands, and the advent of new forms of birth control. Now, in the last half of the twentieth century, as we have become aware that few new land frontiers remain, we are reevaluating his theory.

Malthus has gained recognition not because his theory was original, but because he based it on scientific facts rather than conjecture. He is also regarded for his cogent insight into the many implications of continued population growth.

Like Adam Smith, Malthus did not believe in governmental or other forms of interference. He opposed remedial legislation and various proposals for the redistribution of wealth (a popular notion of the time), maintaining that the natural order of things should not be disturbed. Proposals for improving the lot of the poorer classes were useless, he argued, for even if wealth were equalized, the high rate of reproduction among the proletariat would reduce the impact of their wages. The lower classes created and perpetuated their own misery. The only solution was the adoption of moral checks on their reproduction.

Charles Darwin read Malthus's discussion of how checks in nature crowded out certain plants and prevented them from spreading. Darwin's interpretation of Malthus's description was that favorable variations in plants and animals were preserved and unfavorable ones destroyed. Darwin extended these ideas which, of course, had great impact on interpretations not only of nature, but of society as well. The policy implications of Malthus's work are now generally regarded as pivotal for society's future. Many societies are now forced to contend with extreme population pressures.

KARL MARX

Two basic problems in modern society had their genesis during the early period of social organization: the unequal distribution of wealth and substantial disparities in available leisure time. These ancient inequities, if not exacerbated by conditions associated with early industrialism and the new capitalism, at least became more visible and thus more apt to be defined as problem areas.

In many respects, those who attempted to work within the framework of the new factory system fared worse than their agrarian counterparts, whose lives were far from pleasant. The Factory Act of 1833 was preceded by the famous "Sadler Report" of the British Parliament. The report documented the negative social consequences of early industrialism, which had been intensified by laissez-faire economic and social theory, and calculated the human costs of the relatively uncontrolled quest for profit. As the factory system used laboring people, it often crushed them with fatigue, despair, disease, and death.

The aforementioned economic and social conditions had a singular effect on Karl Marx, who lived in abject poverty for a period of time. He was born in the German town of Trier in 1818. After studying law and philosophy in his homeland he emigrated to Paris, where he studied economics and became a friend and collaborator of Friedrich Engels. He was expelled from Paris when he became a socialist revolutionary, and after moves to numerous European cities he settled in London in 1849.

Marx experienced and understood the impact of laissez-faire capitalism on workers and their families. His writings are an interpretive reaction to poor working conditions, poor living conditions, and other repressive and inhumane facets of the Industrial Revolution. His particular analyses have been heatedly debated and all kinds of evil charged to the influence of his work, but the early industrial and class difficulties (the latter a function of the economic order) to which he addressed himself are no longer questioned by knowledgeable historians.

Marx differed from many Western social scientists in that his work lay squarely in the Vertlos tradition: the starting point was

KARL MARX

23

man. Others could observe, collect data, and add sophisticated dimensions to stratification theory, as they later did; Marx would describe and prescribe. Indeed, there are those who would disqualify him as an important sociologist primarily because sociology is viewed as a method of discovering. In Marx we have a man who "knew."

Marx was known variously as a journalist, philosopher, and economist. Generally, however, his writings deal with social thought that, although too close to philosophical dimensions for disciplinary purists, cannot be denied a role in the effort to understand man and his institutions. Works like *The Communist Manifesto,* written in 1848; *Das Kapital,* written in 1867; and *The Economic and Philosophical Manuscripts,* written in 1844, but published after his death, demonstrate Marx's interest and facility in the social sciences, history, and philosophy. They raise some distinctly sociological questions that even today remain at the center of sociological debate.

Although notable in terms of conflict, change, and alienation, Marx's work is also significant because it involves optimism and hope. Whatever judgments are made of his work, the man remains an intellectual titan of our age.

For Marx, economics represented the basic institution of society. He believed that the way in which a society produces and distributes economic goods determines the balance of its institutional order. Even the ideas that men hold are expressions of economic interest. Economic power, which he defined as control over the means of production, converts into power in other societal institutions such as education or religion and serves the ideology of the capitalist class. He related this economic determinism to the role of ideas in history and to social change and conflict as they affect historical development.

Of special interest to sociologists are the theories of social class set forth in *Das Kapital* and in *The Communist Manifesto.* These treatises examine history in the context of the rise and fall of social classes, an evolutionary process that Marx saw throughout history. He predicted that an ultimate struggle would take place between the proletariat, who were the wage workers, and the bourgeoisie, the capitalists. The conflict would be resolved in favor of the proletariat, who would then establish a classless and communistic society. Dahrendorf, a later Marxist thinker, criticized Marx's preoccupation with property arrangements and attributed the conflict between rival groups to the struggle for authority rather than property.

Current thinking is that Marx's predictions were partially correct: correct for the social environment of the Industrial Revolution but not, of course, correct in the long run. For example, Marx predicted that with the spread of industrialization the social classes would diverge even further. The lower class, he said, would develop a greater consciousness and become increasingly antagonistic to the upper classes; the middle class would lose its status and become part of the proletariat. Since his time the classes have probably become less distinct in both ideology and possessions. The middle class in particular seems to have survived with increased strength in the industrialized world, where the need for managers and middlemen has increased. Even the lowest classes have become cognizant of their stake in the existing system. Marx anticipated that wage earners would spearhead a communist revolution in the more industrialized countries. Of course, he did not foresee the mediating influence of industrial unions or the increased role of governmental intervention in labor disputes. Communist expansion seems to have occurred in the more agricultural economies such as China, or through military conquests; yet reports from Russia and other communistic countries indicate that Marx's classless society has failed to come about. There exist a number of social classes differentiated according to party loyalty and positions of official power. However, there are now indications that Marx's predictions might have some validity in European countries such as Italy. The recent rise of consciousness among blacks in the United States has also lent new credence to the Marxian framework. An important variable seems to be the extent of polarization of the classes.

Marx's hypotheses have served as a base for several comparative studies on institutions in Marxian and non-Marxian countries. His writing is essential to those who seek to understand the pursuit of power and status. Labor scholars have studied the societal conditions that mediated his predicted conflict and revolution of workers. Dahrendorf and Coser have emerged as the leading sociological proponents of a modified Marxian view of conflict in society. They view society as an arena of conflicting groups and classes, but they differ from him in their analysis of the root of the conflict.

VILFREDO PARETO

Vilfredo Pareto was born in 1848 in Paris, where his father, an Italian exile, was then living. He earned a degree in engineering from the Polytechnical Institute in Turin, Italy, then pursued a career in engineering, first with the Italian rail system and later as a superintendent of iron mines owned by an Italian bank. While in this second job he became interested in economics.

The unscientific state of economics as compared to the physical sciences prompted Pareto to develop a new economics more solidly based on scientific method and rationality. His economics was limited to an analysis of logical human action aimed at solving problems associated with scarce resources. Rationality was to be the cornerstone of his economic theory. Pareto's business experiences, however, taught him that economics could not cope with the nonlogical or nonrational elements of human action. He felt that a more encompassing discipline than economics was needed in order to study society in more than a general way. He thus turned to other fields, particularly sociology and psychology, in an attempt to build a scientific economics and to gain deeper control and understanding of the variables that introduced nonrational elements into that discipline. In 1894 he assumed the chair of political economy at Lausanne.

Pareto interpreted society as a social system and created a framework for the ideas of later sociologists such as Talcott Parsons, Robert Merton, and George Homans. The bulk of Pareto's sociology can be found in his *Treatise on General Sociology,* which has been translated into English and reprinted in part in *The Mind and Society,* edited by Arthur Livingston.

There is disagreement as to whether Pareto should be considered a member of the functionalist school of sociological thought. Suffice it to say that he attempted to develop a general

VILFREDO PARETO

27

functional theory of social structure, one that emphasized the more formal properties of theory construction and viewed society as a mechanism of adaptation of man to his environment. Using equilibrium theory based largely on conceptions from physical science, such as those of William Gibbs in chemistry, Pareto attempted to delineate the social system.

In his view society consists of elements that act on it and are in turn reacted upon by it. He classified these elements into three broad groups: (1) climatal, geological, and mineralogical elements; (2) elements external in space and in time; and (3) elements internal to the system, such as ideas, sentiments, attitudes, and knowledge. From these groupings he gathered a more comprehensive list of societal elements. Four of these constitute his basic conceptual scheme for societal analysis: interests, or goal-oriented elements; social heterogeneity and circulation, which comprise class and mobility elements; derivations, which he divided into the four categories of verbal utterances, assertions, appeals to authority, and rationalizations; and residues, which represent predispositions to action.

The question of why societies cohere and endure was of great interest to Pareto. To answer it he carefully examined the changing balance between residues in society, concentrating on two key residues—combinations and persistence. He characterized men of combinations as "foxes," men of persistence as "lions." The foxes were men of experiment, innovation, not above fraud or swindle, in general sly and cunning. The men of persistence, the lions, reacted to them, using physical force if needed; they represented attributes of strength necessary to complement the intellectual thrusts of the foxes. The lions would gradually assume importance while the foxes were ruling and vice versa. Thus, Pareto viewed society as continually shifting and readjusting, but ultimately in a state of stability.

His theory of "the circulation of elites" is probably the most enduring aspect of his sociology. It has been of interest to sociologists such as C. Wright Mills and to political scientists. He studied the formation of elites and their interactions with each other and with the masses. These ideas were continued in the work of William Kornhauser, who developed a number of theoretical propositions concerning elite-mass relations in society.

Pareto's view of society has also been useful to industrial sociologists and psychologists. Working out of a model based on scientific management and the economic motivations of workers, researchers were temporarily puzzled to find that many aspects of work behavior could not be explained with existing rational models. The antirational bias of Pareto's observations of social behavior, especially the notion of sentiments, suggested an alternative approach and established new directions in management.

Talcott Parsons, the leading contemporary exponent of general system theory, admits that he has been influenced by the many valuable insights contained in Pareto's work.

GEORG SIMMEL

Georg Simmel was born in Berlin in 1858 and spent most of his academic career at the University of Berlin. Like many other early sociologists, Simmel's formal study was in philosophy. His dissertation was on Kant's philosophy of nature. His continued interest in Kant is manifest throughout his sociological thought.

Simmel was a prolific writer. The bulk of his published work dealt with questions in moral philosophy and the philosophy of history as well as with Kant, Schopenhauer, Nietzsche, and other thinkers whose writings were influential in Germany and Europe during his lifetime. Sociology in Germany emerged from an examination of social variables by philosophers, economists, and historians. It differed from the perspectives that emerged in France and England. Simmel disagreed, for example, with Comte and Spencer who viewed society as a reality external to individuals and determinative of their behavior and consciousness. According to Simmel, sociology consists of the study of forms of social interaction. That which is social comes into being, he said, only when two or more individuals interact; hence individual behavior can be understood only in terms of the behavior of another to whom the individual is responding.

In *Philosophy of Money* Simmel examined the consequences of the transition from an economy based on exchange in kind to one based on the monetary unit of exchange. In addition to

GEORG SIMMEL

analyzing its obvious influence on the conduct of trade and commerce, Simmel defined money in terms of its function within society. He studied the exchange of money as a form of social interaction and equated the social relationships brought about by the rise of a money economy with other features of modern society. The use of money as a medium of exchange fostered rational calculation in social relationships and was for Simmel the key to understanding the increased rationalization of society. Money exchanges depersonalized relationships between merchants and traders, employers and employees.

The influence of Kant on Simmel's sociology can be seen in the latter's idea that any aspect of social behavior can be studied in terms of both its content and its form. He suggested that forms of social interaction have properties of their own which cannot be deduced from the needs and motives of individuals. The task of formal sociology, he proposed, is to study the conditions under which forms of interaction arise, are maintained, and eventually disappear. Also of concern to Simmel were the lesser or more fleeting forms of social interaction, such as relationships between leaders and followers in small groups, rivalries, and secrecy.

At least two discussions in the 1908 book *Soziologie* have proven to be of lasting value: one on the significance of numbers in social life, the other on conflict. Especially helpful to students of small group research and social psychology is Simmel's discussion of the need for new group mechanisms—division of labor, communication mechanisms, and new forms of authority distribution—as a group increases in size. The relationship between numbers and social life still has not been completely explored.

In viewing social conflict primarily in pathological terms Comte and Spencer were well within sociological tradition. Simmel, however, maintained that conflict is a part of many social relationships and may even promote group stability. Conflicts, he pointed out, generally entail a continuing relationship between adversary parties; indeed, external conflict serves to maintain group life by making the group more cohesive. Simmel noted that the absence of conflict is not necessarily an indicator of the stability of groups or social relationships.

Although Simmel never received recognition as a sociological giant, American sociologists Park and Burgess relied heavily upon him in their *Introduction to the Science of Sociology.* More recently, Kurt Wolff's translation *The Sociology of Georg Simmel* and Coser's *The Functions of Social Conflict* have helped place Simmel's sociology into proper perspective.

HERBERT SPENCER

Herbert Spencer, born in England in 1820, is viewed as a forerunner of modern sociology in that his analogy between society and biological organisms has found its way into much of current sociological theorizing. Spencer received little formal education and did not actually systematically study many of the subjects he wrote on. For a while he was editor of the English publication *The Economist,* but eventually he decided to earn his living through independent writing.

Spencer taught that society, like a biological organism, was composed of a number of parts which performed specialized functions. As examples of these parts he offered the family, political organizations, and various other social institutions. He believed that society was held together by the complex interdependence of these parts. Just as a body becomes sick or dies when a major part is not functioning properly, society withered when its parts or institutions did not function properly.

The ramifications of Charles Darwin's *Origin of Species* are apparent in Spencer's writing. He used Darwin's theory of organic evolution to formulate a theory of social evolution. Spencer saw social evolution as a set of stages through which all societies progress. The stages entail development from the simple to the complex and from the homogeneous to the heterogeneous. As a result of society's evolutionary growth, its parts become increasingly specialized in response to the demand for efficiency presented by increased division of labor. His thoughts here are somewhat similar to Durkheim's description of organic solidarity. Like Comte, Spencer was optimistic that society was moving in a more humane direction.

Spencer saw sociology as a unifying science among the social sciences; the unification of knowledge is a consistent theme in his

HERBERT SPENCER

33

work. His writings were relevant for his time in that they developed justifications for the laissez-faire principle and its associated economic system, which prevailed in England and the United States. It is said that the industrial leaders of the time warmly supported and received him. Among Spencer's major works are *Social Statics* (1850), *The Study of Sociology* (1874), and the classic three-volume work *Principles of Sociology,* written from 1886 to 1896.

GABRIEL TARDE

Gabriel Tarde was born in Sarlat, France, in 1843. He studied law at Toulouse and Paris and spent the early part of his working life as a magistrate. His sociological genius emerged in connection with the practical problems he was called upon to investigate in that capacity. Rather late in his career, at the age of fifty-seven, he was appointed professor of moral philosophy at the Sorbonne.

Tarde's major sociological treatises include *Laws of Imitation* (1890), *Social Logic* (1894), *Universal Opposition* (1897), and *Social Laws,* which summarized the three previous volumes. The process of imitation was the subject of much of his sociological inquiry. Here he followed the tradition of Cournot, the French mathematician, who recognized the need for measurement and classification of recurring phenomena. Tarde characterized scientific inquiry by three processes: repetition, opposition, and adaptation. He attributed all resemblances to repetition, which takes various forms, depending on the nature of the phenomena being discussed.

Social phenomena, he believed, could ultimately be reduced to the relationship between two persons, with one being the dominant mental influence. Society, then, is the result of one man patterning his behavior on that of another. He explained the social process of repetition through a pattern of invention-imitation: Inventions were imitations of former inventions, usually in new or different combinations. The social adoption of inventions is accomplished through imitation, said Tarde, who viewed society as a group of men in imitation of each other.

Tarde's legacy to sociology is limited primarily to his theory of imitation and to his explanations of why some ideas or models

GABRIEL TARDE

35

are adopted and others are not. Although evolutionism was
beginning to sweep sociological theorizing at the time of Tarde's
writing, his ideas were used as an argument against it. His
discussion of imitation was used to explain societal similarities as
well as the diffusion of cultural elements.

His theories were respected by the American sociologist E.A.
Ross, but major figures like Franklin Giddings and Emile Durkheim opposed him. The latter objected to the implications of
individual rather than societal explanation of behavior. Nevertheless, in emphasizing the active role of individuals in shaping society, Tarde's work helped form a tradition of sociological inquiry.

FERDINAND TOENNIES

Analytic sociology flourished near the end of the nineteenth
century. A prominent intellect during this period was the German,
Ferdinand Toennies. Throughout his entire academic life Toennies (1855-1936) held only one post, at the University of Kiel.

The field of social organization as we know it today rests
squarely upon the first and perhaps most important writing of
Toennies, *Gemeinschaft und Gesellschaft,* published in 1887.
Like many German philosopher-sociologists, Toennies was occu-
pied with an analysis of human will. He used this subject as a base
in *Gemeinschaft und Gesellschaft.* He saw all social relations as
creations of either essential or arbitrary human will. The
orientations of these two types of human will are opposed. Essential will is a basic, instinctive tendency that drives human
activity, while arbitrary will is a purposive form of volition that
determines human activity with regard to the future. He applied
this to social interaction and characterized different types of
people by one form of will or the other. Commoners, peasants,
artisans, children, and women were more likely to display essential
will, while the upper class, entrepreneurs, scientists, and men were
dominated by arbitrary will. Clearly, the sociology of knowledge
must be used in defense of the male chauvinist position implied
herein; again we see a theorist being blinded by the culture he
was observing.

The distinction between essential and arbitrary will is crucial
to Toennies's *Gemeinschaft-Gesellschaft* continuum of social or-

FERDINAND TOENNIES

37

ganization of groups. He believed that social groups are willed
into being for different reasons. One group may be willed into
being because its members feel that the relationship is of value in
itself; another may arise because of its instrumental value. The
first type of group is an expression of essential will and is termed
Gemeinschaft; the second is an expression of arbitrary will and
is termed *Gesellschaft.* Present-day sociologists equate *Gemeinschaft* with community or communal groups, while *Gesellschaft*
denotes association or associational society. Toennies analyzed
the family and village neighborhood as examples of *Gemeinschaft*
and the city and the state as examples of *Gesellschaft.*

The evolutionary theories that were so popular in early
twentieth-century sociology appear to have affected Toennies. His
discussion of *Gemeinschaft-Gesellschaft* also seems somewhat
Marxian in orientation. *Gesellschaft* was seen as an emergent
form of social relationship, one that resulted from the separation
or emotional severance of individuals, services, and behavior from
the underpinning of *Gemeinschaft.* Like Marx, Toennies applied
this analysis to the marketplace. Toennies advocated *Gemeinschaft,* a return to kinship and community, as the only genuine
form of living together as human beings. Given the pace and
complexity of modern, urban, industrialized society, and the
frustration and alienation linked to such a social order, it is
understandable that the work of Toennies remains popular today.
The quest for community is a search for identity in an increasingly
complex society.

Early threads of social psychology and perhaps sociometry can
be discerned in Toennies's ideas on social formations. He considered all formations to be products of either essential or arbitrary will. A social relationship exists when two persons will it.
Their objective in doing so could be the preservation or the over-
throw of existing social order. The former he saw as a relationship of reciprocal affirmation, one that sociology should encourage.
Within this framework he wrote of the circle, the collective, and
the corporation, all of which could take a form based on either
essential or arbitrary will.

Toennies is also regarded for his study of social norms. His
classification of normative behavior was superseded by that of

William Graham Sumner, but closely related to his social group typology. It contained the same order and *Gemeinschaft* biases as Toennies's other work.

LESTER F. WARD

Lester Frank Ward, an American, was an early contributor to the sociological tradition, although he never formally studied sociology. After military service in the Civil War and civil service with the United States Treasury Department, he studied botany and law. He later served as chief paleontologist in the United States Geological Survey, where he pursued research interests.

Ward read various sociological treatises coming out of Europe, notably Tarde's work on imitation and Comte's ideas on the role of the sociologist. He wrote a critical treatise on some of this work, selecting those theories with which he agreed, especially those that emphasized psychic forces.

Central to Ward's work was the theory of evolution, which he referred to as "the law of the aggregation of matter." His unit of sociological analysis was social force or energy, with emphasis on the individual act of creative imagination. Social structures, he contended, arise, evolve, and change through a combination of dynamic action, which has a psychic base and a creative imagination. In 1883 he published *Dynamic Sociology,* which called upon sociologists to guide social progress through intelligent social action.

Heavily influenced by the writings of Comte and Spencer, Ward accepted an evolutionary point of view—but one that justified human interference in evolutionary forces. He distinguished between genesis and telesis, the former being blind forces of spontaneous evolution; man's purposive action based on knowledge of the situation and anticipation of the consequences of his action he called telesis.

Hegelian influences seem to be responsible for one of Ward's most famous postulates: the universal principle of creative synthesis, which permitted the transition from one evolutionary stage to another. He called this principle "synergy."

Progress as a means to happiness and routes to this progress, such as education, were recurrent themes in Ward's thinking. He

LESTER F. WARD

40

was an early proponent of equality in education and greater educational opportunity. His study of psychic factors set the stage for the emergence of the social interactionist approach that dominated early twentieth-century American sociology. He became the first president of the American Sociological Society (now Association) in 1906, at which time he assumed his only academic post, this being at Brown University, seven years prior to his death.

MAX WEBER

An inspiration to modern sociological thought and practice, Max Weber (1864-1920) was born in Germany. His early training was in economics and law at the Universities of Heidelberg and Berlin. Unable to endure the rigors of normal academic life, Weber labored as an independent scholar throughout most of his career. His writings are numerous and touch the fields of economics, philosophy, religion, and sociology, among others.

It is impossible to detail all of Weber's contributions to the sociological perspective. Perhaps the most outstanding are his appreciation for the role of ideas in the stream of history; his examination of bureaucratic organization and the process of bureaucratization; and his analysis of the Protestant Ethic and its relationship to capitalism.

Some scholars have interpreted Weber's work as an ongoing questioning of Karl Marx's ideas, possibly because Weber's writing accents the independence of ideas in the development of history. In the area of social stratification, however, he did not necessarily attempt to refute Karl Marx, but sought instead to draw attention to possible alternative explanations. Indeed, most of Weber's work is characterized as a search for explanatory variables in examination of a given social phenomenon. Although Weber agreed with Marx about the struggle between workers and capitalists, he did not see this struggle as the complete explanation of history.

Following Marx's theoretical leanings, Weber believed that ideas were conditioned by material interest, but he also spoke of "ideal" interest. To modern interpreters this means that people are complex creatures with many interests, not all of which can be explained in economic terms. Interest in any social institution, therefore, could be real and important for the individual outside of the economic implications involved.

Weber's most widely interpreted work, the one that has spawned most empirical and theoretical research, is undoubtedly that on the Protestant Ethic and the spirit of capitalism. A basic premise in this theory is that the rise of Protestantism, particularly in its Calvinist variety, was one of if not the most significant independent variable contributing to the rise of capitalism. Like many other writers, Weber was a victim of his own social and cultural context. Possibly, it was a psychological affinity between Calvinism and capitalism that Weber was writing about. He was interested in ideas or attitudes that cleared the way for Western capitalism and demonstrated how ideas inherent in Calvinism contributed to the acceptance of capitalism. The basic tenets of his famous Protestant Ethic are as follows: 1. Work, like money, could be an end in itself, pursued for the greater glory of God or the satisfaction of the individual. 2. Earlier teaching which condemned the use of wealth to acquire more wealth was no longer applicable; thus, proscriptions against usury, a carry-over from the Middle Ages, were seen as inappropriate. 3. At birth every soul is marked for heaven or hell, according to the Calvinist doctrine of predestination, or "calling." Natural inquisitiveness about one's destiny would lead then to self-examination. This introspection would nurture those virtues identified with salvation: work, thrift, sobriety, cleanliness, and other traits.

Weber first attempted to delineate the spirit of Western capitalism, which he compared to the central beliefs of Calvinism. He suggested the following points of similarity:

1. Calvinism is consistent with the spirit of capitalism in calling for active mastery of one's environment. The one system urges mastery in the service of profit or gain, the other in the service of God. The similarity, therefore, is that both ideologies favor activeness.

2. The Calvinist belief in the natural order of the universe parallels the capitalist attempt to interpret the world rationally rather than emotionally. The conviction that reason, science, and applied technology can help under-

Max Weber

43

stand and manipulate the external environment is germane to both Calvinism and capitalism.

3. The individual occupies a central position in both doctrines. Not knowing whether a friend or colleague is among the saved would make one leery of close personal relationships. This detachment is also present in capitalism.

4. Calvinists try to determine salvation from outward signs, primarily success, monetary achievement, and dedication to one's calling.

5. By rejecting worldly pleasure, Calvinists save and reinvest their earnings rather than squander them. This attitude complements capitalism's need to accumulate money for its own sake rather than as a means to some other goal.

Weber offered empirical evidence to link the two doctrines. His observation that capitalism developed and flourished in countries of Protestant rather than Catholic traditions led to his comparative study of religion.

A major theme running through much of Weber's writings is that of rationality, a term that in his writing refers to a particular kind of world view. He was concerned specifically with *Zweckrationell* action: rational action in relation to a goal. There are several steps involved in the general process of *Zweckrationell* action. A person engaging in it first decides upon a goal and then selects appropriate means to reach it. The selection of means is governed strictly by efficiency or utilitarian concerns. In stripping emotionality or mysticism from the decision-making process Weber showed a great affinity with capitalism. Western civilization is conceived of as a world directed towards purposive action, one capable of generating the means to conquer its environment. History studies the direction of rationality as it operates in various institutional spheres.

His ambivalence about rationality is apparent in Weber's study of bureaucracy. He admitted that rationality permitted the most efficient adaptation of means to end, but argued that this efficiency was often at the expense of other elements or processes. He used the bureaucracy, the most efficient means of social organization, to illustrate his point. He characterized it as a soulless mechanism—efficient, but not always adaptable to new situations. The very characteristics that lead to efficiency in a bureaucracy can also prevent it from operating along the desired path.

Weber's analysis of bureaucratic organization enumerated the following distinctive characteristics:

1. Organizational tasks are distributed among the various positions in the organization as official duties. This implies a clear-cut division of labor and a high degree of specialization. Specialization, in turn, promotes expertise among the staff, both directly and by enabling the organization to hire employees on the basis of their technical qualifications.

2. The positions or offices within the organizations are structured hierarchically. In most cases, this hierarchy takes the shape of a pyramid. Within the pyramid, each official is responsible to his superior not only for his personal actions, but also for decisions and actions of his subordinates. The scope of authority of superiors over subordinates is clearly circumscribed.

3. A formally established system of rules and regulations governs official decisions and actions. Typically, the operations in such administrative organizations involve the application of general regulations to particular cases. The regulations insure uniformity of operation and, together with the authority structure, make possible the coordination of various activities. They also provide for continuity in operations despite personnel changes. A stability absent in emotional or charismatic movements is thus obtainable in a bureaucracy.

4. Officials are expected to assume an impersonal stance in their contacts with clients and with other officials. They are expected to disregard personal consideration and maintain complete emotional detachment in dealings with clients and subordinates. The social distance between levels in the hierarchy and between officials and their clients is intended to foster formality. Detachment is designed to prevent personal feelings from distorting rational judgment in the conduct of responsibility.

5. Employment by the organization constitutes a career for officials. Typically, officials are full-time employees who look forward to lifelong careers in the agency. In isolating this trait Weber was clearly a product of his time, an astute observer of the Prussian environment. Employment is based on technical skill rather than on emotional, i.e., political, family, or traditional connections. Qualifications can be determined by examination or by a certificate of the candidate's educational attainment. Educational requirements promote homogeneity among officials, since relatively few working-class people possess these qualifications. Officials are appointed, not elected, to positions, so they are dependent on superiors in the organization rather than on a body of constituents. In such a system, salary is the most common form of remuneration. Individuals often gain tenure in the position and are protected against arbitrary dismissal. Career advancements are earned through seniority, achievement, or both.

In Weber's view, these organizing principles maximize rational decision making and administrative efficiency. Each is designed to encourage efficient operation. Bureaucracy, according to Weber, is the most efficient form of administrative organization. He felt that experts with experience are best qualified to make technical decisions and that disciplined performance governed by abstract rules and coordinated by the authority hierarchy fosters a rational and consistent pursuit of organizational objectives.

Weber's model of bureaucracy was an ideal; we know that reality is somewhat different. His concern was strictly with the formal nature of the mechanism. Bureaucracies, however, are also characterized by an informal structure that functions not only to protect the individual, but also at times to promote efficiency and goal attainment. Later social scientists have done much work on the reformulation of Weber's ideal model. The model has, however, given rise to much empirical study and discussion within sociology. It has helped shape a number of subfields, including complex organizations and industrial sociology.

Much of Weber's writing—on Calvinism, on the spirit of capitalism, and on *Zweckrationell* action—was concerned with so-called ideal types. The ideal type was for him merely exaggeration of certain features of social life.

A study of modern sociological theory or current research in sociology will show the lasting consequences of Weber's writings. His interest in bureaucratic organization and the process of bureaucratization and his appreciation of the dynamics of history and the complexities connecting ideal and real interests are among his most fruitful concerns. He led us in particular to realize that a one-variable explanation of history and social phenomena will always be incomplete.

Chapter 2

The Beginnings in America

Given the diverse origin of sociology as a discipline, its beginnings in America were relatively coherent. Lester Ward's attempts to apply sociology to societal problems, and a general belief in progress, set a tone that was to characterize many of the early efforts here. Theories of evolution and models of Darwinism in the natural sciences provided a framework adopted by early twentieth-century American social scientists, who also studied the psychological aspects of social life.

This section explores the ideas of several American theorists—Charles Horton Cooley, Franklin H. Giddings, George Herbert Mead, Robert E. Park, Albion Small, William Graham Sumner, and William I. Thomas—all prominent in the development of sociology in the United States.

Although Social Darwinism and its theories of evolution have fallen into disrepute, they seem to have held the key to maintaining sociology as a discipline in its infancy in America. Small and Sumner were both Social Darwinists. Small, an important transitional figure, reminded American sociologists of the legacy of their European colleagues, particularly the Germans. He is remembered more for the way he nurtured the discipline of sociology in America than for his theories. Sumner, on the other hand, is noted for his numerous conceptual contributions. He brought a new perspective to the field by drawing attention to the normative aspects of social life.

49

Park, who taught in the University of Chicago's sociology department (which Small founded), made one of the first attempts to apply sociology to the study of urban and community life, focusing on social interaction in the city.

Giddings was an evolutionist, much in the tradition of Ward. Giddings's theories, however, attempted to balance the relationship of individual and society. His writing, as evidenced by his concept of "consciousness of kind," has a strong psychological component. Giddings was a precursor of Cooley and Thomas, who were both interested in the individual's relationship to society. Indeed, this interest prompted Thomas to formulate several important concepts and to bridge the gap between theory and research.

Mead is considered the founder of the symbolic interactionist school in sociology. Like Cooley, his interests were largely in phenomena related to socialization, such as the formation of mind and self. He drew attention to social interaction as a process and to the role of communication in it.

CHARLES HORTON COOLEY

Charles Cooley, who spent almost all of his academic life at the University of Michigan, was an early president of the American Sociological Society. He made a number of substantive contributions, many of which are still significant. Among his writings are three major works: *Human Nature and the Social Order* (1902), *Social Organization* (1909), and *Social Process* (1918).

Two trends apparent in the writings of other late nineteenth- and early twentieth-century social theorists also appear in Cooley's work. These are the beliefs that society is progressive and that it conforms to a pattern of evolution. Cooley's evolutionary ideas, though, highlighted the development of individual social beings or the social self rather than the total historical process.

Cooley viewed history as moving through two channels, one genetic and one cultural, analogous to Ward's conception of genesis and telesis. Pragmatic and psychological theories also shaped Cooley's sociological views; ideas of thinkers such as William James and James Baldwin are apparent in his works. Cooley saw sociology as the study of social relationships as they reflect ideas, attitudes, and sentiments.

CHARLES HORTON COOLEY

51

His view of society represents a convergence and compromise of earlier positions. His conception of society is definitely in the organic tradition; unlike Spencer, however, he did not see the individual as basic and the group as the sum total of parts; nor did he see the group as having primacy over individuals, as Durkheim did. Rather, Cooley recognized the interdependence among societal parts and between society and the individual. He viewed society as a total, composed of differentiated segments, each having a specific function. Society and the individual were collective and distributive aspects of the same phenomenon. His unique organic and psychological view stressed the importance of primary groups in society, of social interaction—especially in the form of communication, and of the development of personality.

In his theory of the "looking-glass self," the self emerges from social relationships; that is, self-development depends upon a person's ability to view and judge himself as he imagines others do. This theory of self-development is basically reflexive: The individual gains a view of his self by assuming the view of others. Cooley formulated three steps in self-development—appearance to others, judgment by others, and resultant modification of behavior. To gauge our appearance to others, it is necessary, in Cooley's view, that language already exist, for others communicate their expectations to us through language. We, in turn, use social standards to judge ourselves. We modify our behavior not only through various voluntary means, but also through social control mechanisms.

Cooley, like George Herbert Mead, studied the process of socialization and the means by which individual perceptions of self and others emerge. He found that early experiences, especially early impressions of how others judge us, are strategic in molding an enduring personality. He saw, too, that early judgments are more durable and more difficult to change than those formed later in life. These observations have been adapted and expanded by contemporary Neo-Freudians. In sum, Cooley viewed the self as a social product. In contrast to Freud, Cooley did not see self and society as being in conflict; and unlike Mead, he accepted self and society as two aspects of the same reality.

Cooley's seminal concept of the primary group spawned research on social groups. He defined primary groups—which exhibit social processes such as conflict and cooperation—as intimate, face-to-face associations that allow an individual to express his personality and sentiments relatively freely. He believed that primary groups foster social progress by instilling in their members universally found social ideals such as the spirit of service and obedience to norms. The primary groups he was most interested in were the family, the play group, and the close neighborhood group. He labeled them "primary" because they generally constitute an individual's first social experience.

In addition to these interests, Cooley wrote on other topics, such as social classes (which he viewed as universal and functional) and the role of transportation routes in the development of cities. His main interests were, however, in the more psychological aspects of sociology, and his influence in this area remains strong.

Franklin H. Giddings

Although he studied engineering as an undergraduate, Franklin H. Giddings embarked on a career in journalism when he graduated from Union College. Journalism provided him with perceptive insights into social life. From this base he first taught politics at Bryn Mawr College, then sociology at Columbia University, where he spent the remainder of his academic career.

Giddings was representative of late nineteenth-century trends in sociology. Following an evolutionist perspective, he probed the psychological aspects of social reality. In the later years of his career he also embraced neopositivism and the movement towards quantification in sociology.

Influences from both Spencer and Ward are found in Giddings's writings. His first major published work was *Principles of Sociology* (1896), in which he adopted a biological perspective and analyzed social evolution as a phase of cosmic evolution. He alternated between psychic and physical explanations of society. Like Ward, he saw society as a psychic phenomenon, but limited by physical constraints. He argued that social laws as precise as those found in natural science could be arrived at. Along with Ward, he be-

FRANKLIN H. GIDDINGS

lieved that the key element in social phenomena was volitional in nature.

Giddings's principle of consciousness of kind, akin to Adam Smith's concept of reflective sympathy in social life, posited a state of consciousness wherein humans recognize one another as being of like kind. When this recognition takes place, individuals experience common emotions and act in concert. The social mind, maintained Giddings, is a result of the interaction of consciously united individuals, a product of the simultaneous mental activity of two or more individuals in communication with one another. This concept is reminiscent of Durkheim's collective mind. The principle of consciousness of kind became the base of Giddings's sociology, which he set in a framework of evolutionism.

Using historical and retrospective methods, Giddings approached sociology as the study of the evolution of mankind to its contemporary state. He regarded it as a concrete science generating principles about all social phenomena. It was to him an encompassing science that studied the attributes common to all subclasses of social reality. He saw the psychic process as the basic social process, bounded by physical processes.

Giddings divided his sociology into (1) statics and kinetics and (2) dynamics. He then divided statics into social composition and social constitution. The former referred to unconscious groupings in society and the latter to the conscious organization of societal members into groups to achieve social ends. His concept of statics delineated social (elite), nonsocial (masses), pseudosocial (dependent persons), and antisocial (criminal) classes. Also subsumed under statics is the concept of tradition, which we would now equate with culture.

The notion of social kinetics demonstrates the influence of Social Darwinism on Giddings. Conflict is an important general mode of action in kinetics, and in connection with it Giddings introduced the concept of toleration. He was convinced that no superior strength could emerge from periodic social conflict. Thus, he saw toleration as the result of conflict and force.

As opposed to statics, dynamics approximates function in more contemporary interpretations. Giddings reduced dynamics to the study of social genetics and processes of human evolution. He suggested that in its evolution toward progress society passes through four stages: zoogeny, anthropogeny, ethnogeny, and demogeny. Relating this concept to consciousness of kind, he postulated that favorable responses to like individuals trigger a volitional process in which some persons are selected to survive, while others are rejected. Although he emphasized volitional choice, Giddings pointed out that nature, too, sometimes rejects the harmful elements of society. Darwinian thought permeates Giddings's sociology. He recognized community standards that surround choice, but he also understood the physical limits placed by natural selection and survival.

While at Columbia, Giddings met Richmond Mayo-Smith, a statistician who convinced him of the need for quantification in sociology. In his later years Giddings shifted from a historical to a statistical method and began to favor a behavioristic approach.

Though he agreed with Spencer on many points, Giddings rejected the notion of society as an organism. His emphasis on psychic aspects of society was more akin to the ideas of Ward, Cooley, and Thomas. Parsons, of course, carried on his view of sociology as a more general science.

GEORGE HERBERT MEAD

George Herbert Mead was born in 1863 in the town of South Hadley, Massachusetts. Both his father, a minister with puritanical tendencies, and his mother enjoyed and encouraged intellectual pursuits and achievement.

Mead graduated from Oberlin College and later became a student at Harvard, where he came under the influence of pragmatic philosophy in the person and works of William James. He did not earn a doctorate at Harvard, but he later continued his formal studies in Leipzig and Berlin. He married Helen Castle in 1891, and in the same year became an instructor in the Department of Philosophy and Psychology at the University of Michigan. At the request of the highly respected John Dewey, Mead joined the faculty of the University of Chicago in 1893. During his tenure there he was most productive in socialization analyses and in suggesting paths for empirical investigation.

GEORGE HERBERT MEAD

57

Though a lucid and persuasive teacher, Mead published very little during his lifetime. Even his famous *Mind, Self and Society* was published posthumously. Fortunately, the products of his brilliance were preserved by a number of distinguished colleagues, admirers, and students, including John Dewey, W. I. Thomas, Ellsworth Faris, T. V. Smith, and Herbert Blumer. Mead is overshadowed by many in terms of academic accolades, but his intellectual legacy cannot be overlooked. His inquisitive, searching, analytical mind and his apparently genuine humility made him a truly remarkable scholar and an exceptional human being.

Mead, who as a social psychologist established a line of inquiry now pursued by social interactionists, is an important forerunner of sociological thought on socialization and the development of the self. His framework was somewhat similar to Charles Horton Cooley's theory of the looking-glass self. Both view the self as arising in a social context through an appraisal of the judgments of others.

In *Mind, Self and Society* Mead drew attention to the role of language in the development of the self. By allowing a person to determine how his behavior in specific situations or roles is regarded by others, language builds images of how others are judging his behavior. In so doing, it provides a base for one's own judgments about his behavior. With language, the individual can predict the extent of reward or punishment to expect from others as a result of his actions.

Mead's theories on the development of personality are akin to Freud's in stressing the importance of particular persons such as parents in the early life of the individual. Once the child makes judgments as to what will be regarded as appropriate or inappropriate behavior, he can then indulge in role playing, praising or punishing himself in the language of his parent. Like Freud, Mead saw other individuals replacing the parent in the child's hierarchy of priorities as he develops. Mead termed the commonalities in the judgments of these others "the generalized other." The child, he said, adjusts his concept of self according to his generalized other, which represents the external world. As he anticipates societal approval or disapproval of his behavior, he begins to make moral judgments. He bases decisions regarding his behavior on his perception of society's overall reaction to this behavior. As the child internalizes a morality, he acts less on anticipated reward or punishment and more on his evaluation of the rightness or wrongness of an act. The transfer of judgments from parents to others to society is, according to Mead, essential in the development of an internal morality.

Mead's work on the development of self is relevant for the study of social control. The child, he argued, will learn that expectations depend upon an individual's position, not his specific identity. Evaluation is based on how well one fulfills societal and individual expectations of behavior in a role. These expectations or norms governing roles facilitate everyday social interaction. Reward for conformity and punishment for norm or role violation can be understood in this context. The criminal, for example, can contribute to social solidarity by reminding nonoffenders of the rules of society and thus helping them to form a consciousness of kind and values.

Mead's work remains very much a part of the interactionist perspective in the analysis of society and social problems.

ROBERT E. PARK

Robert Ezra Park became interested in sociology after an early career in journalism. As a journalist, he concerned himself with social problems and their resolutions, particularly urban problems and conditions that led to the oppression of black Americans. He served for a brief time as a secretary to Booker T. Washington.

A leader of the great Chicago school of sociology, Park undertook a number of community studies on aspects of urban ecology and social interaction. In general, his writings conveyed a pessimistic view of urban life. He noted the lack of primary group ties in cities and accented the more negative aspects of apparent disorganization.

In his analysis of the city, Park followed a model somewhat akin to Durkheim's system of social facts. Park viewed the city as a natural phenomenon, a product of largely random, undesigned, uncontrollable forces organized into various areas such as manufacturing, business or commerce, and residence. He ob-

ROBERT E. PARK

served that individuals of similar economic and cultural traits tended to aggregate in specific areas of the city, and that the social and cultural characteristics of each area tended to be superimposed on the life styles of the inhabitants. In collaboration with Ernest W. Burgess, he was among the first to employ the term "human ecology." He and the ecologists who followed him correlated various social and cultural phenomena with so-called natural areas of the city. In particular, they associated social disintegration with slum areas and with what they referred to as the zone of transition.

Park devised the concept of marginal man in the course of his studies on assimilation. He intended the term for individuals who were on the fringes of two groups or two ways of life, not fully belonging to either. This conceptual breakthrough has now been applied to individuals of mixed racial ancestry and to the foreman in a traditional factory organization.

Introduction to the Science of Sociology, written by Park and Burgess in 1921, was a respected textbook during the early period of American sociology. It was primarily a classification and analysis of social processes, a term the authors applied to recurrent patterns of social interaction. They felt that society could be understood only through an awareness of the major social processes found in all groups and societies. These processes include cooperation, competition, conflict, and accommodation.

The process of assimilation, particularly the assimilation of racial and ethnic traits in American society, received much attention in Park's writing. His description of the caste aspects of ethnic groups can be linked to William Lloyd Warner's discussion of social stratification.

Park is acknowledged as a prominent figure in the development of empirical research in American sociology.

ALBION SMALL

It can be said with certainty that of the early sociologists in America, Albion Small (1854-1926) was the most instrumental in fostering sociology as an intellectual enterprise. Although he published several books, Small is remembered not for his theories, but for his reflections on sociology as a discipline and his dedication to that cause.

Small's early academic interests were history, economics, and theology. After graduating from the Baptist Colby College in Maine, he studied at the Universities of Berlin and Leipzig. The impact of this training, particularly his study of German social science, remained visible in Small's writing and thinking throughout his lifetime. His Ph.D. was in welfare economics, a subject he later taught at his alma mater, Colby. He became president of Colby at the age of thirty-five, but two years later, in 1891, he joined the University of Chicago, where he founded the first sociology department anywhere in the world. He continued in this direction, founding both the American Sociological Society and the American Journal of Sociology.

In 1905 Small wrote *General Sociology,* a book that familiarized Americans with European, especially German, social theorists. The work also introduced his theory of interests—the conflicts they engender, and their resolution in society. He equated interests with desires, which he considered the mainspring of human activity, a view similar to that of Lester Ward. Small contended that interests were the simplest modes of motion in human activity. In fact, he saw social life itself as a process of acquiring, adjusting, and satisfying interests. In the final analysis, he identified society with the sum total of individual attempts to satisfy interests. His sixfold classification of interests—health, wealth, sociability, knowledge, beauty, and rightness—reflects the influence of the Austrian sociologist Gustav Ratzenhoffer.

The process of human association was another key concept in Small's study of society. Again, following Ratzenhoffer, he focused on conflict and the collision of individual interests. In his analysis, though, conflict was not problematic to society, for it could generally be resolved into cooperation through socialization. He joined Comte and other early sociologists in taking a positive view of society and its members. Ratzenhoffer's influence is again apparent in Small's belief that society progressed as it resolved conflicts over interests. Both men discussed society's evolution from a conquest to a culture state.

ALBION SMALL

63

The Meaning of the Social Sciences presents a plea for viewing the various social sciences in a unified way. This interdisciplinary perspective, Small argued, would allow sociology to pursue objective investigations of the process of association. His work also exhibited a humanistic bias in that he felt it incumbent on the sociologist to make human life all it could possibly be—using objectivity as his guiding principle. Small supported the idea of state socialism and was enthusiastic about the place of Karl Marx in social theory. In fact, he compared Marx in social science to Galileo in physical science.

Much of Small's writing contains a theme that derives from moralistic philosophy. Much of it also represents an attempt to bring the benefit of earlier European thought to America and to place these thinkers in a sociological perspective. For example, in *Adam Smith and Modern Sociology* Small captures the sociological significance of Smith's economic doctrine. He regarded *Wealth of Nations* as a sociological work that drew attention to the economic processes of society and thought it unfortunate that sociology did not pursue the social analysis implicit in Smith.

Few aspects of Small's work hold any significance today; yet one must acknowledge that his encouragement and support helped fashion American sociology. During his lifetime he supported sociological giants like Ward, and many of his ideas, notably his theory of interests, can be traced in the works of theorists like MacIver.

WILLIAM G. SUMNER

William Graham Sumner was born in Paterson, New Jersey, in 1840. Although his family was rather poor, having immigrated to the United States from England, Sumner managed to journey to England and study at Oxford. His early scholarly inquiry tried to determine whether a science of society was indeed possible.

Sumner was an adherent of Spencer's evolutionary theories. His entire academic career was spent at Yale University, where he rose from the rank of tutor to that of full professor. He succeeded Lester Ward as the second president of the American Sociological Society.

WILLIAM G. SUMNER

His only principal work, *Folkways,* was conceived as a prelude to a major volume, *Science of Society,* which he never completed. Albert G. Keller, who succeeded him at Yale, later finished the book and published it under both his and Sumner's name.

For Sumner, evolution was the basic law of society that science was to study. He accepted it as an irreversible force, propelled by man's struggle for existence and the resultant competition. He preached survival of the fittest, with the fittest being the most industrious, frugal members of society. Like Marx he noticed class struggle throughout history.

Folkways was an attempt in the style of Social Darwinism to explain the origin, function, and persistence of group life and habits. He distinguished between folkways and mores. The former are commonly accepted way of doing things that develop unconsciously in society; the latter are the result of the development of some folkways into more binding doctrines. This distinction is useful for understanding of small group structure and functioning. Sumner's name is associated with the beginnings of the normative approach to social behavior, an approach developed by Talcott Parsons and others eminent in current sociological study.

In *Folkways* Sumner also originated the concept of ethnocentrism, which identifies a significant factor in racism and intergroup relations. He applied the term to the tendency to judge other groups according to the standards of one's own group. Ethnocentrism exhibits two tendencies: (1) a tendency to regard the standards of one's own group so highly that they become the sole criteria by which other groups are judged and (2) a tendency to regard the culture of other groups negatively and to perceive them as out-groups. This second aspect seems to be involved in what we commonly refer to as prejudice. Sumner's distinction between we-groups and they-groups is a counterpart to ethnocentrism.

Other terms attributed to Sumner include "crescive change" and "antagonistic cooperation." The first refers to the fact that what mores command at one time may be frowned upon later. The second refers to the way in which social groups sometimes arrive at accommodation by allowing each other to disagree without open conflict or fighting.

Sumner's contributions to sociological terminology and to the direction of the field cannot be disputed, but his ideas on survival of the fittest, origins of folkways, and law as reflective of the mores have been refuted.

WILLIAM I. THOMAS

William I. Thomas is considered to be one of the first important American sociologists. He was born in Virginia in 1863 and studied at the Universities of Tennessee, Berlin, and Gottingen, Germany. He was one of the first students in the newly established Department of Sociology at the University of Chicago. He later taught at Chicago, the New School for Social Research, and Harvard. Thomas was an independent scholar who devoted large amounts of time to nonuniversity-based research.

His major published works include: *Source Book of Social Origins,* also published under the title of *Primitive Behavior; The Polish Peasant in Europe and America,* the grand-scale study on which he collaborated with Znaniecki; *The Unadjusted Girl,* published in 1923; and *The Child in America.* Some of his theories appear in a volume entitled *Social Behavior and Personality,* edited by Edmund H. Volkart and published by the Social Science Research Council.

Thomas was most interested in the concept of social organization, defining it as a network of institutions which, when viewed collectively, constitute a set of rules imposed by social groups upon their members. Social action, the action of an individual in a social situation, was his fundamental unit of analysis. Sociologists today still respect his theory that social action is determined by the actor's definition of the situation and by a combination of objective conditions, attitudes, and values acquired by the actor over time.

Thomas was a psychological sociologist, sensitive to the interaction of society, culture, and personality. He tried to understand the differences in behavior and culture among social groups by studying the life experiences of these groups. He added another dimension to the differences through a psychological interpretation of them. His study of the Polish peasant reinforced this perspective.

Thomas made an enduring contribution to the methodology of the social sciences in applying to that discipline the same rules of logic operative in the physical sciences. He concluded that the most relevant procedure for the social sciences was to be found in the situational approach, which analyzes the conditions that determine an individual's actions in a total situation. He advocated measurement and tabulation of the statistical frequency of social behavior and urged the use of control groups. Research documents were invaluable to his methodology, for they helped him understand how different factors integrated meaningfully in an individual's life. Again, *The Polish Peasant in Europe* is an excellent illustration of his use of documents.

Thomas's work is still regarded as the classic example of the use of case study methodology in social science. Much of our knowledge about delinquency stems from his case study in *The Unadjusted Girl* and cogent insights into personality disorganization have emerged from his collaborative work with Znaniecki. The latter work is also pertinent to the study of assimilation and the Americanization of new citizens.

Conceptually, Thomas made a number of contributions to the field of sociology, the most prominent being the terms "definition of the situation" and "self-fulfilling prophecy." By the former he meant that social reality is only what it is defined to be by the participants, an attribute often neglected by empirical researchers. In effect, Thomas was suggesting that it is not reality or truth that determines much of man's behavior, but rather a subjective social or cultural definition of reality. In a statement often referred to as the W. I. Thomas theorem, he argued that "if men define situations as real then they are real in their consequences." The theorem is basic to the study of social processes and has been extremely useful in explaining such diverse behavioral manifestations as those associated with race and sex.

The self-fulfilling prophecy, now recognized as a social mechanism for producing specific forms of behavior, is an outgrowth of the Thomas theorem. As a case in point, femaleness as socially or culturally defined has meant inferiority. Institutional patterns

WILLIAM I. THOMAS

and social expectations are geared to this definition and are reinforced by a system of rewards and punishment (negative and positive sanctions). Through time, the individual belonging to a category so defined tends not only to conform, but also to internalize the definition. Thus, the self-fulfilling prophecy contains within itself the capacity to incorporate what was originally a false definition into our accepted reality.

The self-fulfilling prophecy is applicable to areas other than sex and race. Its implications extend as well to the study of life chances as related to mental or physical impairment, class differences, religious orientation, and other social phenomena.

Two other sets of concepts developed by Thomas—the so-called four wishes of man and the three personality types—have received some sociological acclaim, but the extent of their impact is not yet known. The four wishes as outlined and illustrated in *The Unadjusted Girl* were security, recognition, response, and new experience, all of which could be satisfied, Thomas postulated, only through an individual's incorporation into society. Thomas later admitted that there were shortcomings in this typology, for he could not explain precisely how the four wishes related to the formation of an individual's attitudes. Nevertheless, the four wishes, which F. Stuart Chapin later referred to as needs, are still utilized, albeit cautiously, in attempts to explain the motive force behind certain forms of social and antisocial behavior. Senility symptoms, for example, are often attributed to the denial or withdrawal of recognition. The subfield of industrial sociology has also adopted a human relations perspective positing a hierarchy of wishes or needs and linking need satisfaction, motivation, morale, and productivity.

The three personality types described by Thomas were the philistine, the bohemian, and the creative. He admitted, though, that these were ideal types, with characteristics of each type being present in every individual.

Thomas's concept of definition of the situation and his theory of the self-fulfilling prophecy have proven to be enduring and useful in the analysis of social interaction and social processes.

Chapter 3

Sharpening the Focus

Several sociologists and social scientists contributed to the perspective of the developing discipline of sociology. Generally, their contributions either moved the discipline into new areas of inquiry or sharpened the role it played in subfields that were already established. The ideas discussed in this section are examples both of additions to substantive content and of methodological breakthroughs.

Research into the community began to attract sociologists' interest during the 1920s, and it continues to be a focal point of sociology today. Those who helped develop the sociological component of community research, and who are discussed in this section, include Robert Lynd, who studied Middletown; Ernest Burgess, the architect of the concentric zone model for the study of cities and one of the first to examine human ecology; William F. Whyte, William Lloyd Warner, and August B. Hollingshead, all of whom studied various aspects of social organization and related them to societal phenomena or problems.

In general, most of the early concerns in sociology involved an attempt to make the seemingly familiar more understandable. The family, work, and social change were prominent topics of analytic inquiry among pioneer theorists like Burgess, William Goode, Everett Hughes, Reinhard Bendix, William Ogburn, and Karl Mannheim. Some sociologists maintained that social organization could be best understood through the study of its opposite

—social disorganization. Edwin H. Sutherland, creator of the differential-association framework for the study of criminal behavior, was among the first to venture this opinion.

Upon examining the structure of American society, a number of sociologists were surprised at the prevalence of social stratification and class consciousness. This section looks at William Lloyd Warner's classic work in the Yankee City series, the structural functionalist approach to social stratification developed by Kingsley Davis and Wilbert Moore, and some of the empirical studies that used social class as an independent variable in explaining societal phenomena.

Like most other disciplines and occupations, sociology did not develop without internal soul-searching as to the nature of the discipline and the proper role of its disciples. C. Wright Mills offered one of the most cogent examinations of sociology as a discipline. Although some consider him contemporary, we include him in this section because his writing influenced the direction of the field itself.

While sociology was broadening and sharpening its substantive thrusts, a number of practitioners were furthering its methodological development. Lynd, using observation for the most part, presented an initial model for the study of community life; Whyte developed observation into a respectable scientific technique in *Street Corner Society*. Warner and Hollingshead, in addition to their theoretical interests in social stratification, designed scales for the measurement of social class. Neopositivist concerns, addressed here in the sketches of F. Stuart Chapin and George Lundberg, forced sociology to devise more sophisticated measurement and design techniques. In response, a quantitative methodology evolved which was to hold a place with traditional qualitative approaches like Florian Znaniecki's use of life documents, discussed in this section.

After reading this section, one should not hold the impression that early and mid-twentieth-century sociology was strictly a series of empirical studies. Attempts to generalize theories from this research were a part of the ongoing development. One of the leaders in the attempt to generate societal theory was Pitirim Sorokin. A discussion of his work is included in this section.

REINHARD BENDIX

Born in Berlin, Germany, in 1916, Reinhard Bendix received all his education in sociology at the University of Chicago. He earned his Ph.D. from that school in 1947 and subsequently taught there. He was also a faculty member at the University of Colorado and a research sociologist in the Institute of Industrial Relations at the University of California at Berkeley. In 1958 the American Sociological Association awarded him its prestigious MacIver Award, and in 1969 he was elected to the presidency of the organization.

In the book *Work and Authority in Industry*, Bendix, operating in a Marxian tradition, explored questions concerning subjection and submission of workers and the ideologies that foster these processes. The work is significant not only for the fields of the sociology of work, and industrial sociology, but also for the sociology of knowledge. Basically, he sought to explain the ideological differences between totalitarian and nontotalitarian economic enterprises. To do so, he compared managerial ideologies around work and workers in England, tsarist Russia, the United States, and the Soviet Union and its satellites. In addition to its substantive content, Bendix's book is valuable for its comparative methodological framework.

Bendix has been identified with cross-societal work. "Political Sociology," an article he coauthored with Seymour M. Lipset in *Current Sociology,* pointed out that the relationships among variables in political sociology had generally been analyzed only in connection with specific political events in a given country. Intrasocietal relationships show variation when they are viewed cross-societally, the authors maintained. In particular, they examined upward mobility and tendencies toward conservatism; social class and support of leftist political parties; professions and their political leanings; and voter turnout, social class, and social integration —all on a cross-societal basis. They again used cross-societal data in *Social Mobility in Industrial Society.* In this case, data was gathered from the United States, Japan, and various European countries to illustrate that the amount of social mobility, as measured by intergenerational occupational mobility, is compara-

REINHARD BENDIX

74

ble in all industrial societies, although the nature and direction of their mobility rates can vary. The measure of social mobility used in this study, a nonmanual classification, was somewhat crude.

Finally, in "Modern Society," a chapter in *American Sociology,* Bendix used comparative data from England, the United States, and the Soviet Union to define the term "modern society." He demonstrated how differences in the process of modernization produced different structures in these societies and pleaded for an interpretation of modern society that embraced the actual experiences of societal inhabitants.

Conflict is a recurrent theme in Bendix's writing. It appears, for instance, in *Work and Authority in Industry,* which examines societal inclination toward revolution in the context of ideological structure, and in his translation of Georg Simmel's *Conflict.*

ERNEST W. BURGESS

In sociology, Ernest Burgess has become synonymous with the traditions of the Chicago school. Along with Robert Park and Louis Wirth, he produced a wealth of sociological materials on urban life and culture which not only sharpened the focus of sociology in the 1920s, but also made a lasting impact on the field.

Burgess is identified as one of the founders of the ecological approach in sociology. In their general textbook, *An Introduction to the Science of Sociology,* he and Park helped to launch the study of human ecology. In the 1920s he developed the concentric zone model, the first to study urban spatial structure. It used Chicago as an example and originally assumed that all cities conformed to the same general pattern. The model began with a central business district, the heart of the city. Surrounding this district were rings or zones of light manufacturing, lower-class residences, and then more middle-class residences. According to this model, social status increased with distance from the central city; moves away from the central district to the outer zones of the city represented upward social mobility. As part of his model, Burgess discussed the zone of transition, a decaying and disorganized area undergoing rapid social change. He pre-

ERNEST W. BURGESS

76

dicted that as the zone of transition went through the change process, new zones would be added to the city, thus diminishing the status of the older zones. The concentric zone model received much attention and stimulated much research in mid-twentieth-century sociology but was later replaced by the sector model and the multiple-nuclei model.

Burgess's later works reflect the influence of the Chicago tradition in sociology. In 1960 he published *Aging In Western Societies,* a cross-societal study of the relationship between the generations. Even in this context, Burgess suggested a reexamination of the concepts of isolation and anomie in urban areas. His studies of the relationship between social development and kinship solidarity posited a linear model: Tradition societies are characterized by high kinship solidarity and some form of an extended family structure, while urban industrial societies are characterized by a decline in kinship solidarity and simple nuclear structure. A more prevalent sociological model for the examination of the relationship between urbanization, kinship solidarity, and family structure is the curvilinear model. This model concedes that a highly developed kinship system is absent in both the simplest and the most complex societies.

Burgess's work in ecology, urban sociology, and family studies has enriched the sociological perspective and remains relevant today.

F. STUART CHAPIN

Like William Ogburn, F. Stuart Chapin was an early twentieth-century sociologist who studied at Columbia University under Franklin Giddings and later promoted neopositivist theories in American sociology. Chapin, who spent most of his career engaged in teaching and research at the University of Minnesota, applied statistical methods and experimental design to sociological research into housing and social and cultural change.

Contemporary American Institutions, his major written work, described social institutions as patterns of human behavior which consist of conditioned responses, habits, and attitudes. He relied heavily on graphs and other visual aids to illustrate the hidden patterns of interconnectedness between and within these institu-

F. STUART CHAPIN

tions. Chapin urged sociologists to apply units of standardized measurements to the study of social institutions. To this end he and his students invented scales for the accurate recording of phenomena such as social status, family life, family size and the effects of housing.

Methodologically, Chapin was an advocate of the experimental model, which he borrowed from the physical sciences. Since social scientists cannot possibly hold states of social change steady, he proposed that they observe two or more states of the social system or condition that differ according to the presence or absence of the factor thought to be of causal significance. This approach was developed further by Ernest Greenwood in his *Experimental Sociology.* Chapin also demanded operational definitions of research variables in order to insure the objectivity of the researcher's design. This emphasis on operational definitions led to the neopositivist insistence on scales of measurement.

In *Social Change,* his second major work, Chapin discussed cultural maturity and called upon sociologists to be aware of the development of culture. A culture, he stated, is composed of group cultures exhibiting cycles of national ascendency and decay. Each cycle is the product of the growth and decline of individual phases of culture, such as social institutions. The nation or group experiences its era of maturity when combinations of cycles reach their pinnacle simultaneously. Though interesting, this explanation is not complete because it does not identify which or how many cultural traits must be taken into account when assessing differing cultures. However, Chapin's framework did help move social theory away from evolutionism by focusing on the interdependence of cultural and social parts.

KINGSLEY DAVIS

Born in Tuxedo, Texas, in 1980, Kingsley Davis has become a widely recognized world expert on population change and structure, social and demographic factors in economic development, and functionalist sociological theory. He received his Ph.D. in sociology from Harvard University in 1936 and has held positions at such prestigious universities as Princeton, Columbia, the

University of California at Berkeley, and the University of Southern California. He was elected president of the American Sociological Association in 1959 and of the Population Association of America in 1962.

In 1949 Davis published *Human Society,* which adopts a strong functionalist perspective and pursues a number of theoretical leads from Talcott Parsons. Davis advocated an equilibrium model of society, wherein the various parts work together to maintain a balanced state.

One of the best-known aspects of Davis's sociology is his collaborative effort with Wilbert Moore on social stratification. Davis and Moore are identified with the structural functionalist viewpoint on stratification and the allocation of roles in society. They maintain that social inequality, although arrived at unconsciously by societies, insures that the important positions in society are filled by the most highly qualified individuals. They consider some institutionalized form of social inequality as inevitable, contending that societies must differentiate persons in terms of both prestige and esteem. From this perspective, social stratification is a result of societal rather than individual needs. The authors note uniformity in the amount of prestige awarded to the main types of positions in similar societies. Prestige decreases as one descends the stratification ladder. Finally, Davis and Moore point out that societies, depending on their complexity, their main means of production, their value systems, and other factors, will adopt stratification systems that differ in degree and type.

The Davis and Moore thesis grew out of the equilibrium perspective, for they sought to develop a model of stratification that would account for both universal and variable aspects of the phenomenon. Their model complements their broader theory that the components of social systems seek to maintain the system. Society in the model is maintained through proper and efficient role performance. Individual members of society must internalize its goals and be motivated by them in role performance. Societies must have a storehouse of rewards sufficient to motivate people to fill the necessary social positions and to perform the concomitant functions acceptably. According to Davis and Moore, society must dis-

KINGSLEY DAVIS

81

tribute rewards differentially because the positions vary in importance and demand different skills and preparation. In this schema, rewards are built into positions.

The structural functionalist approach to stratification highlights society's needs and neglects aspects of individual motivation caused by personality and psychological factors. It does not adequately address individual differences in role performance. It assumes that there are universal criteria for defining every position in society and for selecting individuals to fill those positions, and it neglects ascription.

Apart from his work with Moore, Davis has conducted studies of population and demography. His theory of demographic transition explores the pattern of relationship between birth and death rates in world population. He has published several major studies of urbanization patterns in non-Western societies and has assessed urbanization's effects on social institutions, particularly the family.

Davis's functionalist perspective has given him unusual viewpoints on several social issues. His analysis of prostitution, for example, points up its salutary effects on family life and society. By allowing individuals to enjoy sexual variety while remaining monogamous, prostitution strengthens marriage and family ties, he argued.

The functionalist perspective is widely used in mid-twentieth-century sociology. Davis has applied it to a far-reaching array of social concerns and must be considered one of its most thorough proponents.

WILLIAM J. GOODE

Born in Houston, Texas, in 1917, William J. Goode has added to the sociological perspective a series of studies in social organization and social structure. In particular, he is considered a leading theorist on the family as well as on religion and social control.

In 1963 Goode wrote *World Revolution and Family Patterns,* a challenge to the hypothesized impending disintegration of family structure. Goode postulated a worldwide trend toward conjugal family structures but noted that this movement is not always apparent to observers because each society is developing from a different direction and at a different rate. In this work Goode presented an ideal model of the conjugal family. It includes extended kinship ties, neolocal residency, mate choice, and descent. In addition to presenting descriptive materials, Goode urged sociologists to investigate how urbanism and industrialization relate to the movement toward conjugal family structures. This challenge has prompted numerous cross-societal, comparative studies.

Goode studied the influence of urban and industrial conditions on the family in Africa, Japan, India, China, and the Arab world, treating the family variable as a causal as well as a dependent factor. He modified existing theory, which held that the conjugal family is a function of industrialism. He showed how change in family structure is partially a function of change in ideology and values independent of industrialization and its consequent increased differentiation.

Goode continued the theme of the relationship between industrialization and the trend toward conjugal family structures in his text *The Family*. Here he stressed the central importance of the family as a social institution throughout the world. "The Sociology of the Family," one of the chapters in *Sociology Today,* outlines the classic structural functionalist approach to the study of institutions.

Much of Goode's theorizing is drawn from cross-societal study. His analyses of comparative data on love, divorce, illegitimacy, and religion contain valuable methodological and substantive lessons for sociology. Sociology cannot progress as a discipline unless its followers are prepared to go forth from their own familiar surroundings to test their observations in other contexts.

Goode created the concept of role strain to refer to a situation in which conflict arises from contradictory expectations that are built into a role. For example, the policeman must be friendly and helpful to young children in order to inspire their confidence and respect for the law, but he also must be stern with them if they violate the law.

Goode has taught at Columbia University in New York for many years. He has received the coveted MacIver Award of the American Sociological Association and was elected to the presidency of that organization in 1971.

AUGUST B. HOLLINGSHEAD

August B. Hollingshead received his Ph.D. in sociology from the University of Nebraska. He taught at the Universities of Iowa, Alabama, and Indiana before becoming the William Graham Sumner Professor of Sociology at Yale University.

Hollingshead's research interests follow questions of social structure, delving most deeply into the areas of social stratification, health and illness, and the community.

His first important published work was *Elmtown's Youth* (1949), a classic study in the sociology of education. Written in the tradition of the earlier Chicago community studies, this one links two important social institutions: the school and the social stratification system. It establishes and documents a correlation between the social class of families and the treatment of their children in the school system. The research which he conducted as a basis for *Elmtown's Youth* set a pattern for Hollingshead's future work.

With the psychiatrist E. C. Redlich, Hollingshead pushed further into empirical research on the social stratification system and its relationship to other social phenomena. Hollingshead and Redlich coauthored *Social Class and Mental Illness,* an analysis of incidence, type, severity, and treatment of mental illness according to social class. It also addressed the relationship between social mobility and mental illness. While examining the relationship of social class to mental illness, Hollingshead and Redlich refined important methodological devices for measuring social class. They pushed beyond a univariate approach and devised a multiple-item index of social class based upon occupation, education, and residential location.

Hollingshead continued the interests of *Social Class and Mental Illness* by moving into the study of differences in attitude toward psychiatry, differences in family structure and types of mental illness (schizophrenia in particular), and different societal approaches to illness.

The focus of sociology did indeed expand due to Hollingshead's work. The sociology of education, the sociology of mental health, and the field of social stratification all received a significant impetus from his empiricism. Familiarization with Hollingshead's studies will allow scholars to develop a broader understanding of social structure and its consequences.

EVERETT C. HUGHES

Everett C. Hughes received his Ph.D. in social anthropology from the University of Chicago. He has taught at a number of major universities, including McGill, Chicago, Brandeis, and Boston College. He served as president of the American Sociological Association from 1962 to 1963 and is honorary lifetime president of the Canadian Sociological and Anthropological Society.

Although Hughes's interests span a wide spectrum in sociology, his major research is concentrated on race and ethnic relations, especially concerning French Canadians, and the nature of professions and professional education. *French Canada in Transition* is perhaps his most famous work, along with a classic essay, "Dilemmas and Contradictions of Status," which appeared in the *American Journal of Sociology* in 1945. Among his other publications are *The Sociological Eye: Selected Papers on Work, Self, and the Study of Society; Men and Their Work,* which contains excellent documentation on the ways individuals and entire professions attempt to gain autonomy in their work; and *Boys In White,* of which he is a coauthor.

The sociology of work owes a great debt to Everett Hughes. His numerous descriptive accounts of work and theoretical abstractions about it have moved American sociology from simple interest in the worker's life outside the work place to a deeper concern with the experience and meaning of work. He has documented the history of numerous occupations in terms of their movement towards professionalism. His studies are especially useful today, in an age characterized by continual emergence of new occupations and competing claims for autonomy and work control. He has aided sociology in its attempt to make analytical distinctions between occupations and professions and between science and profession. Although he subscribes to the existing formal definitions of the term "profession," he has also made us aware of the working definition, that is, an attempt to upgrade occupational prestige.

Everett C. Hughes

Hughes's theoretical examination of social stratification resulted in his coining the term "status inconsistency," which he used to describe the phenomenon whereby an individual ranks high on one dimension of status and low on another. As an example, Hughes pointed to the predicament of the black physician. Status inconsistency, he said, can be resolved if the members of society can agree on the relative importance of the various status hierarchies in their stratification system.

Much of Hughes's early work is a good example of the use of descriptive anthropological methodology. His writing and procedures are excellent documentation for the argument that there is unity in social scientific knowledge.

GEORGE A. LUNDBERG

A former president of the American Sociological Association and long-time professor of sociology at Washington University, George Lundberg was the most influential sociologist of the neopositivist tradition in mid-twentieth-century American sociology. His major works are *Foundations of Sociology* (1939) and *Can Science Save Us?* (1947), both of which set forth the neopositivist approach.

For Lundberg, science was the barometer used to judge the validity of all knowledge. He viewed science as an adjustment technique, and his interpretations followed the tradition of behaviorism. He saw inquiry as always beginning with an experienced tension, or strain, in the inquiring organism; from this point of view, adjustment approximates a state of equilibrium, or normalcy. All phenomena of scientific concern, Lundberg maintained, consist of energy transformations in the physical cosmos. Motion, or energy transformation, occurs in a field of force equivalent to that aspect of reality defined as "the situation." A certain parallel with the ideas of W. I. Thomas can be seen in this emphasis on "the situation." Social science finds its subject matter in the movement, or behavior, that determines one's position in social situations.

Lundberg's approach to the study of social interaction and communication is based on analogy with biochemical stress, restoration of equilibrium, and the attraction and repulsion of atomic particles. He claimed that quantification of sociological principles and generalizations was a necessity if sociology were to be regarded as a science. In *Social Research,* Lundberg recommended measurement of attitudes through scales. An emphasis on behaviorism reinforced his demand for quantification. In his view, attitude becomes that which is measured by a specific scale or research tool. An example of this is his famous definition of intelligence as that which the I.Q. test measures.

Many argue that the operationalism advocated by Lundberg represents an extreme view. Yet it is certainly not extreme to demand that definitions be based on empirically verifiable attributes of that being measured.

HELEN & ROBERT S. LYND

Robert and Helen Lynd coauthored two pioneer studies on American culture and community life: *Middletown* and *Middletown in Transition.* The first was published in 1929 and the latter, which expanded and updated the earlier study, in 1937. These works effectively demonstrated the extent of the type of survey that sociological methodology could undertake.

In both studies, the Lynds were breaking new ground in that they were attempting to produce a so-called total situation effort. In the first volume, the Lynds compared the situation of the town in 1925 to what it had been in 1890. (The town employed for this research, it is now known, was Muncie, Indiana.) The Lynds were particularly interested in social life occurring in six general activity areas which they referred to as "trunk activities": getting a living, making a home, training the young, using leisure in various forms, engaging in religious practice, and engaging in community activities. They subsumed all of life under these six headings but admitted that their studies had a number of shortcomings, such as their apparent value biases. They contended that they were simply describing small town life as they experienced and observed it.

Although the Middletown studies have inherent weaknesses, such as their rather simplistic two-class conception of stratification, they are interesting and important insights into the nature of social life generally. They offer enlightening commentary on the power and class structures of town and city life and cogent analysis of the relationship between power and the class structure. The studies are still frequently cited in current sociological literature. Certainly, the Lynds' use of participant observation, interview, and document analysis techniques is instructive.

Robert Lynd's classic treatise, *Knowledge for What?* (1939), broadened the sociological perspective by raising a series of questions about the nature of American culture and the role of social science in shaping the future of that culture. It points to inconsistency and strain in various characteristics of American culture. For example, he explains the difficulties in attempting to live within the framework of a culture that entails important—yet antithetical—assumptions which are frequently internalized, thus producing ambivalence and cultural confusion. Though he views science as instrumental in helping man understand and shape his cultural surroundings, Lynd presents a critique of the purpose and method of social research.

Not only does Lynd take issue with those who insist that social scientists can and should be free of value considerations and thus be nonethical and objective; he also legitimizes the advocacy of values. In contrast to those who uphold ethical neutrality in the interest of scientific objectivity, Lynd believes that the sociologist, who is professionally trained, experienced, and thus—supposedly—knowledgeable about the nature of the social order and social problems, should suggest values to society. To do less would, in Lynd's opinion, deny others the value of the sociologist's expertise. To do less would be an abdication of the responsibility of formulating policy.

At the time *Knowledge for What?* was written, Lynd was acutely aware of the serious problems that confronted man. These ranged from the erosion of faith in progress to the implications of Hitler's growing power. Lynd was greatly concerned about the accelerating rate of change in society and about the potential dysfunctions rapid change could bring. It was precisely the critical nature of many social problems of the time that prompted him to suggest the promulgation of values.

Although contemporary, mainstream sociology demands scientific objectivity, few would seriously argue that the scientist is capable of assuming a totally value-free stance. Conversely, many question the wisdom of suggesting values, arguing that the discipline would become hopelessly fragmented and that there would exist as many sociologies as there are sociologists. At any rate, the debate continues, and Lynd's point of view is still respected.

Given the seriousness of many contemporary problems, it is likely that Lynd would agree with those who believe that "In not taking a position, one takes a position,"—which implies that neutrality, as far as values are concerned, represents support for the status quo.

In retrospect, it is quite likely that Robert Lynd's work is notable for its suggestion of what sociology could become rather than for its content.

KARL MANNHEIM

To evaluate the sociology of Karl Mannheim, one must employ the tenets of the sociology of knowledge which he so fondly advocated; that is, one must evaluate his theory in light of the social, cultural, and historical forces that held sway during his lifetime. Intrinsic to Mannheim's plan for society is an elite intelligentsia. This elite, though it would be attentive to the needs of the masses, would not succumb to what Mannheim perceived as the negative consequences associated with the rise of these masses.

Born in Hungary in 1893, Mannheim lived through the Bolshevist uprising and counterrevolution that swept that land. He was one of the restless youths who challenged the authority of the ruling intelligentsia and rose to some influence in the revolutionary government. The situation in the Hungary of his early manhood made a lasting impression upon him, and he came to believe that it was possible to reassert the role of reason in society and to apply intelligence to the resolution of society's problems. His ideal was a society in which the masses of peasants and workers, though autonomous, would operate under the guidance of a creative and cohesive body of intellectuals.

KARL MANNHEIM

91

From Hungary Mannheim went to Germany. There he developed his own sociology of knowledge, using Marxist theory as a starting point. He set forth his ideas in his 1929 work *Ideology and Utopia.* Its theme echoes Mannheim's belief that every social position carries its individual perspective. The sociologist should identify and analyze these perspectives in order to locate the social roots of ideas that demonstrate the relationship between ideologies and social situations.

Mannheim showed his bias for the intelligentsia in maintaining that its members are in a position to understand and evaluate the solutions or partial explanations of reality yielded by various and competing perspectives. He considered the intelligentsia to be emotionally detached, objective in its own perspectives, and thus in a position to analyze the totality of reality or truth. This seemingly naive belief in the power of the intellectual has provoked criticism of Mannheim.

The question Mannheim seemed to address was how consensus could be achieved in society. He advocated an integrated, cohesive society in which social change would be effected by the intelligentsia. He was convinced that sociology, as an active science, could mitigate the negative aspects of inevitable social change by controlling and channeling it to maintain a state of dynamic equilibrium.

After the appearance of *Ideology and Utopia,* and following the rise of Hitler to power, Mannheim was forced to flee Germany for England. He progressed beyond the concept that ideas result from perspectives that are themselves shaped by social positions and began to examine the role of social processes in the creation of ideas. He also moved from his Marxist emphasis on the role of social classes to analysis of other social units such as age cohorts and generations. Mannheim began to develop what he later referred to as "sociology of the mind." Regardless of the unit of analysis, Mannheim never abandoned his faith in planning or in the possibilities of applied sociology. He called for a reemphasis on the primary group and a rediscovery of its potential for education and socialization. Due to increased interest in the sociology of knowledge, Mannheim's impact is greater today than it was during his lifetime.

C. WRIGHT MILLS

C. Wright Mills was a leading critic of both sociology and American society in the mid-twentieth century. He studied sociology under Hans Gerth at the University of Minnesota; he later collaborated with Gerth to edit *From Max Weber* (1946), which contains an informative biographical perspective on the man. Mills, who taught at Columbia University, pursued a social interactionist framework based heavily on Weber and Spencer, but he also accepted a Marxist perspective.

Interests in social psychology and political sociology characterize Mills's writing. Along with Gerth he published *Character and Social Structure,* a book that reflects the influence of both George Herbert Mead and Sigmund Freud. Gerth and Mills used the concept of social role to unify the sociological and psychoanalytic perspectives. Role emerged as a central concept in their view of society as a structure composed of numerous institutional roles. They analyzed the total social structure in terms of institutional orders such as the economic or political. They offered four alternative principles which supposedly foster societal integration: correspondence, coincidence, coordination, and convergence. Using these four alternatives they constructed theoretical propositions concerning societal integration.

Mills wrote a number of influential volumes, including: *The New Men of Power* (1948); *White Collar: The American Middle Class* (1953); *Power Elite* (1956); *The Sociological Imagination* (1959); *Images of Man* (1959), a selection of writings on sociologists of the classical tradition; a vigorous support of Castro's power play in Cuba entitled *Listen Yankee* (1960); and *The Marxists* (1962), a short treatise on Marxist sociological thought.

White Collar has proven to be an important impetus to research in the subfield of the sociology of work. This volume presented a rather pessimistic analysis of the station of white-collar workers as well as general insights into work and its meanings. Mills documented how status, a central concern of workers, can lead to what he called "status panic." On this point he probably also had the discipline of sociology in mind. The concern with status rests on the assumption that real power does not exist in inter-

C. Wright Mills

94

mediary positions in organizations, but resides only at the top. Mills's writing set a tone for later sociologists studying work, for they accepted his assumption that work per se is unpleasant and that workers possess a feeling of fatalism about it. Mills's observations include the notion that blue-collar workers are much less satisfied with their jobs than are white-collar workers. In factories, work has little meaning other than monetary reward. A Marxist influence can be abstracted from these remarks.

Perhaps the most notable aspect of Mills's work is his "power elite" thesis. He used the term to refer to an informally linked group of individuals who exercise major influence over American society. He verified that .02 to .03 percent of the adult population control the largest corporations in the country. This power elite has potential as well as real power. If one assumes that power is concomitant with specific social positions, it becomes apparent that a state governor possesses more power than a minor civil servant in a state bureau, or that the president of the local Jaycees possesses more power than a lone local businessman.

Mills examined the managerial classes in particular, pointing out that managers often control the groups of which they are the nominal servants. He viewed managers as a self-perpetuating group, capable of dealing with boards of directors, trustees, and other officials. He envisioned a professional managerial class in the United States, but other social scientists have not accepted the case for a ruling elite with virtual monopoly over social power.

Though Mills's early death denied him the possibility of seeing many of his social projections become reality, his work continues to have a critical impact on societal analysis.

WILLIAM F. OGBURN

William Ogburn, who studied sociology at Columbia University in the early decades of the twentieth century, undoubtedly formed his ideas under the influence of Franklin Giddings, an early neo-positivist. Ogburn's writing explores the interaction of technology, invention, and culture.

In one of his works, *The Social Effects of Aviation,* he used correlations to chart statistical relationships between technology

WILLIAM F. OGBURN

and economics. He demanded empirical data to reinforce theoretical generalizations and exhorted sociologists to devise methods of predicting future social developments.

One of Ogburn's aims was to shift sociology away from the psychological evolutionism that characterized it at the time toward the study of social change. He also differed from earlier writers in his definition of culture as an accumulation of products of human society.

In his classic work, *Social Change,* he applied the concept of "cultural lag" to the analysis of differing rates of change within rather than between societies. The concept describes the disharmony that arises when related parts of a single culture undergo unequal rates of change. Cultural lags are more common in rapidly changing societies. Outsiders may interpret them as signs of backwardness, but they are merely reflective of the inability of society to cope with rapid change. As an example of cultural lag he recalled that although there was an influx of workers to factories—where they were often injured in industrial accidents—around 1870, not until several decades later did most states begin to enact workmen's compensation laws. Further evidence of the lag of social institutions behind changing technology in the twentieth century is seen in the continued use of paper ballots in some election districts, the effects of urbanization on unemployment, and the notion of societal responsibility for structured unemployment. By assigning technology a leading role in social change, Ogburn aligned himself with Thorstein Veblen. His neopositive leanings are evident in his calls for the measurement of the extent of both cultural lag and its consequent maladjustment.

In addition to the concept of cultural lag, Ogburn's writings contain many innovative hypotheses on social change. He talked of a cultural base of supporting knowledge that makes invention or discovery almost a certainty. He noted also how the same discovery can be made by several people at about the same time. His analyses of radio and aviation pioneered the idea of examining one cultural element or invention to uncover its effects on the broader culture.

In his study of invention he grouped the social effects of invention into three major types. First are the multiple effects of a single mechanical invention, which he called dispersion. This category would include the impact of radio, television, or the automobile on social institutions, on new industries, and on new social roles. The derivative social effects of a single invention he called succession. By this he meant that a given invention produces changes which in turn effect further changes. For example: The typewriter helped speed up the recording of information, which touched off the knowledge explosion, which in turn demanded new methods of printing and reproducing written materials, which called for more skilled, white-collar and office occupations, which led to innovations in office design and changes in the sexual composition of the work force. Convergence denotes the coming together of several influences of different inventions. The settlement of the American West, for example, was hastened by transportation improvements like the railroad and the covered wagon, agricultural improvements in the form of farm implements, and new material comforts.

Ogburn's relevance to modern sociology is questioned by some in the field since his emphasis on diffusion runs contrary to the tenets of functionalism, now a dominant framework in sociology, one that accepts or rejects ideas on the basis of their contribution to the total system. Ogburn's insistence on empirical study and the gathering of supportive data is, however, consistent with recent sociological trends.

PITIRIM SOROKIN

Born into a peasant family in Russia, Pitirim Sorokin became one of the most highly recognized scholars in American sociology. From 1924 to 1930 he chaired the Department of Sociology at the University of Minnesota; he then established one at Harvard University. He was a prolific writer, having published numerous books and hundreds of articles on sociological theory, particularly the examination of broad societal values.

Social and Cultural Dynamics, a three-volume analysis of recorded history from ancient Egypt to the 1930s, is a major addition to the study of social and cultural reality and the processes of change therein. The ideas and methodology contained in these

PITIRIM SOROKIN

volumes were expanded in a fourth volume of this work, published in 1941. It was also a response to criticism of the three
earlier volumes. *Social and Cultural Dynamics* represented one
of the first sociological attempts to quantify qualitative judgments
about the importance of historical events. Basically, Sorokin
searched for eras in history when certain patterns of behavior,
activity, thought, or creativity were predominant. He outlined
these patterns and their effects on individuals and social institutions. When the patterns break up, an adjustment process begins,
said Sorokin, and they are replaced by values, which also eventually
form consistent patterns. Old patterns, though, never disappear
or break up completely. He felt it was the task of the sociologist
to chart and describe the patterns predominant at any one point
in history.

Sorokin saw the period from approximately the sixth to the
twelfth century as dominated by Christianity. Other aspects of
social life, such as art or philosophy, reflected this religious
dominance. Sorokin termed this period "ideational." The pattern that emerged from the confluence of ideas and influences
around Christianity he called a "logico-meaningful sociocultural
supersystem."

He contrasted the modern way of life, which he called "sensate," to the ideational pattern. In the sensate pattern, Scriptures
and holy teachings are replaced by sensory proofs and reasoning
based upon the senses. Institutions such as science shift their base
of knowledge and support. Positivism, pragmatism, and rational
sources contribute to institutional character. Themes of art and
philosophy in the sensate age are based on feelings, emotions,
enjoyments, and satisfactions.

Despite criticism, Sorokin did mold an organized, coherent
system for the interpretation of society. He shaped it not through
ideological whim or armchair philosophizing, but through a careful analysis of historical record. One must marvel at the overwhelming nature of such a task. Sorokin also provided sociology
with a base from which to evaluate its subject matter. Because
society became understandable to him only when its cultural system or base was understood, he called for an examination of the

meanings, values, and norms inherent in a society's institutions and way of life.

Since the roots of sociology extend to Europe, Sorokin's 1928 volume, *Contemporary Sociological Theory,* was invaluable to American sociologists. It presented a detailed history of sociology, indexing several hundred writers and classifying sociological theories according to schools of thought and dominant themes. Sorokin completed a follow-up, *Sociological Theories of Today,* almost forty years later. Meanwhile, several sociological theorists followed the organizational pattern presented in the earlier work.

Additional contributions of Sorokin include his criticism of sociology and its direction in *Fads and Foibles in Modern Sociology and Related Sciences,* and his analysis of social and personality structure in *Society, Culture and Personality.* With the ascendancy of theorists like Talcott Parsons, Sorokin's writing is being reexamined and reread in these later decades of the twentieth century.

EDWIN H. SUTHERLAND

One of America's leading criminologists, Edwin H. Sutherland moved sociological investigations of criminal behavior away from Cesare Lombroso's concentration on the individual characteristics of criminals to an examination of crime as a social phenomenon. This is the thrust of his classic work, *Principles of Criminology,* which in later editions he collaborated on with Donald Cressey.

Sutherland guided sociological inquiry into a new era of criminal behavior: white-collar crime, or crime committed by professional, business, and certain employed persons in the course of their work. He moved beyond the level of the individual criminal and contrasted the ways in which corporate and individual crimes are prosecuted—the former as civil offenses, the latter as criminal offenses. His ideas led to an array of research into the activities of large corporations, an area he identified as important long before the current surge of interest in this topic.

Through his empirical studies, Sutherland arrived at an explanation of criminal behavior based upon an adaptation of learning theory. His theory, which he called "differential association," asserts that criminal behavior is learned in interaction with other

EDWIN H. SUTHERLAND

people. Deviance is conformity to the expectations of one's sub-
cultural reference group. Sutherland's theory has been used to
explain various forms of deviant behavior, as in Erving Goffman's
descriptive account of how a person becomes a marijuana user.
Its main propositions are as follows:

1. Criminal behavior is learned.
2. It is learned through interaction and communication with
   other people.
3. Learning occurs in intimate personal groups rather than
   through impersonal sources, such as media.
4. Learning criminal behavior includes mastering the techniques of crime and acquiring attitudes toward the behavior
   itself; e.g., defining the activity as pleasurable or all right.
5. The specific direction of motives and drives is determined
   by favorable or unfavorable definitions of the legal codes.
6. A person becomes delinquent or deviant when exposed to
   more definitions favorable to violation of law than unfavorable to it. This is probably the most problematic part of
   the theory.
7. Criminal behavior can be an expression of the same values
   and needs as noncriminal behavior. (This point is only
   currently receiving the attention it merits; it counters the
   many explanations that rest upon an all-or-nothing socialization model.)

Although Sutherland's theories circumscribed a narrow area of
social behavior, they do have implications for broader issues. He
drew attention to larger structural issues of society, including
social control and the classic concern of social integration.

WILLIAM LLOYD WARNER

Following a generalized functionalist approach, William Lloyd
Warner sharpened the focus of sociology through his community
studies, with their special attention to social stratification. Blending the sociological traditions of Robert Park with the methods of
applied anthropology, Warner conducted several studies known
as the Yankee City series.

The Yankee City series uses the functionalist perspective to examine the social life and structure of a small to medium-sized

New England town. Throughout the four-volume series one en-
counters the notion that when reciprocal interaction is defined in
terms of social relationships, it produces both formal and informal
groupings. These groupings, or social structures, regulate the behavior of individuals. They are interrelated parts of a larger
dynamic system. Warner recommended an elaborate system of
formal and informal sanctions as a way of regulating these
structures.

The Yankee City volumes deal with the problem of social order
or integration. Warner felt that in any given society integration is
arrived at through one main component. In the community that
he studied and, he thought, in American society generally, the
structure of social class performed the integrative role; the Yankee
City studies thus concentrated on the ways in which social class
influences life in communities. Although somewhat superseded
by newer and more sophisticated measures, Warner's index of
status characteristics, created to operationalize social class in the
Yankee City series, was one of the first real attempts to sort out
the variables that combine to form the elusive phenomenon of
social class.

Warner devised a sixfold classification of social class in Yankee
City. It simply divided each of the existing classes—upper, middle, and lower—into upper and lower levels. This classification
was valid for Warner in his work in an older, fairly typical New
England town and for some older medium- and large-sized cities,
but its relevance has been questioned for newer regions and communities where tradition and family ties are diminished. Nonetheless, it did stimulate the creation of newer and different classification systems.

In his book *American Life,* Warner drew some of his earlier
observations together into a more coherent framework that named
two antithetical principles operative in the American social system:
the principle of equality and the principle of unequal status, or
superior and inferior rank.

Warner's studies have sharpened the focus of sociology in other
areas besides social class. In his work on assimilation of racial
and ethnic groups into the American social system, *The Social
Systems of American Ethnic Groups,* he concluded that assimila-

tion is more likely to occur when minority groups are both culturally and biologically closer to the dominant group. *The Social System of the Modern Factory* demonstrated how workers are affected by their environment. In this case, workers in a shoe factory were alienated by the company's switch from local to distant management and by the introduction of mass-production methods. When the workers felt that their status and integration into the community were being undermined, their skills deteriorated.

William Lloyd Warner's work opened up new areas of investigation and demonstrated how general concepts could be abstracted from descriptive empirical studies. It paved the way for an era of consciousness in research methodology.

WILLIAM F. WHYTE

William F. Whyte's intellectual pursuits extend from the 1940s into the 1970s. He received his Ph.D. in 1943 from the University of Chicago and subsequently taught there, at the University of Oklahoma, and at Cornell University. He now serves as director of the research center at the New York State School of Industrial and Labor Relations at Cornell.

Whyte has applied sociological and anthropological insights to cross-cultural study, particularly to the study of social change and development. His interdisciplinary approach has been substantively and methodologically productive. Substantively, he has added to our knowledge of organizational behavior through his study of human relations in the restaurant industry, factors associated with the motivation of workers, and the role of the manager. Methodologically, his name is synonymous with participant observation and field techniques.

Street Corner Society, his detailed account of life in a white, working-class, mainly Italian section of Boston, holds valuable lessons for anyone planning to undertake an observational study. First published in 1943, the landmark study challenged a long-standing view of urban life as disorganized and lacking in social organization. Whyte's astute description of the social organization network of the "corner boys," and of their neighborhood-level links to organized crime, presented an image of inner-city life not previously found in the literature. Methodological issues addressed by Whyte in this work include: the identification of oneself as a sociologist when gaining entry into social groups; the interaction between a researcher's image and the nature and range of the data shared with him; the dependability of informants; and the effect of a researcher's participation in the group on both the group and the study.

In recognition of his field work expertise and his thoughtful analysis of human organization, Whyte was elected president of the Society for Applied Anthropology in 1964. The recent emergence of applied sociology should enhance the value of his contributions.

LOUIS WIRTH

Louis Wirth (1897-1952) was Robert Park's student at the University of Chicago. Wirth, too, became a professor at Chicago and continued the traditions of Park in studies of communities and the social life of Chicago residents. During his career, he refined the sociological perspective on minority studies and urbanism.

Although Wirth wrote most often about the negative characteristics of urbanization, such as anomie and social disorganization, he did subscribe to an order model of society, seeking to isolate the factors that promote cooperation among people in communities. His two best-known published works are *The Ghetto* and "Urbanism as a Way of Life." The latter, an article that appeared in the *American Journal of Sociology,* provides an excellent overview of the Chicago school of sociological thought.

Wirth believed that there existed a culture of urbanism, spawned by a combination of factors such as population size, density, and heterogeneity. He commented on the transitory, impersonal, segmented nature of the relationships among urban dwellers. He also discussed the commercialization and rationalization of activities in cities and the diminished attention paid to family and other primary groups in urban areas.

Students of Wirth also directed their analyses toward the more negative aspects of city life—social disorganization, mental health problems, and distrust of the social environment. Their accounts built a base of knowledge for contemporary urban sociologists to

LOUIS WIRTH

107

work from, but recent scholars agree that there is more structure and organization in urban areas than was suggested by Wirth and the Chicago school. By and large, they did not account for ethnic or class differences in adaptation to city life, or for the fact that some city residents prefer urbanism while others are trapped by it.

Wirth distinguished four types of minorities based on his study of goals and interactions between minority and dominant groups: pluralists—who wish to maintain their identity in a nation composed largely of minority groups; assimilationists—who wish to submerge their minority identity and blend into the dominant culture; secessionists—who wish to be politically independent from the larger society; and militants—who wish to dominate other groups.

Much of Wirth's work has been superseded by newer and more complex descriptive studies, but his early investigations serve as a base for these newer studies. The rise of the new field of urban studies is a tribute to Wirth and the tradition he represents.

FLORIAN ZNANIECKI

We have already discussed Znaniecki's collaboration with W. I. Thomas on *The Polish Peasant in Europe and America.* The men began working together when Znaniecki, who was born in Poland in 1882, came to the United States at the outbreak of World War I. He settled in America many years later and became president of the American Sociological Society in 1953.

Znaniecki differentiated between culture and society, using action as the basic unit of analysis. Most significant in Znaniecki's schema are conscious behaviors that influence individuals or collectivities. These he classified into creative, reproductive, and destructive. He related action to his more general postulate of "universal cultural order," the theory that actions are culturally patterned and result in regularly realized outcomes and purposes. He termed the integration that arises from functionally interdependent actions an "axionormative system."

The psychological component of Znaniecki's work is apparent in his concept of the "humanistic coefficient" and his study of conscious and selective aspects of human action. The humanistic

FLORIAN ZNANIECKI

109

coefficient explains the importance of human consciousness both for the individual and for society. It highlights individual attitudes and evaluations of life occurrences, as evidenced by the importance that Znaniecki assigned to personal documents in his research.

Znaniecki's opinions on symbolic communication and the receptivity of individual mental states are widely held in sociology today. His work parallels Cooley's in recognizing the interdependence of individual and society, and his notion of culture as a system composed of systems is reminiscent of Sorokin and Parsons.

Chapter 4

Enhancing the Focus

The province of sociology has been enlarged by substantive and methodological advances in allied social and behavioral sciences. While analytically distinct from these sciences, sociology shares with them the desire to explain and understand reality. Thus it is that the subject matter of science cannot be neatly packaged into distinct disciplines.

The individuals acknowledged in this section represent a few of the many nonsociologists who have shaped the discipline. Under assessment here is the work of Gordon Allport and Kurt Lewin in social psychology; Ruth Benedict, Bronislaw Malinowski, Margaret Mead, George Murdock, and Robert Redfield in anthropology; John Dewey in education; Sigmund Freud, Erich Fromm, and Thomas Szasz in the psychoanalytic tradition; Robert Michels in political science; and Gunnar Myrdal and Thorstein Veblen in economics.

The discipline is indeed richer for their work. Let us hope that sociologists continue to be receptive to the work of our colleagues in other disciplines and that we not pretend to possess a monopoly on the knowledge of social reality.

GORDON W. ALLPORT

The hybrid field of social psychology has enriched sociological theory by providing us with another basis for understanding individual motives and behaviors within social groups. One of the foremost contributors from social psychology has been Gordon W. Allport, best known for his research on the nature of attitudes, the nature and consequences of prejudice, the basis of rumor, and its effect on social movements.

Psychologists concern themselves with attitudes and attitude measurement. Sociologists examine the social consequences of attitudes and the social contexts in which attitudes develop. Working from both perspectives, Allport explained how attitudes structure one's orientation to social reality. He defined them as learned states of readiness—a potential for behavior—and traced them to various sources, generally social in nature.

The study of race and ethnic relations has been enriched by Allport's 1958 book *The Nature of Prejudice,* which details the origins, process, and consequences, both individual and societal, of prejudice. The book analyzes the psychodynamics of prejudice from the point of view of the social implications of aggressive behavior involved in scape-goating and projection. It also looks at how people react when they are denied equal access to social rewards and opportunities.

Allport suggested that victims of discrimination will express their frustration in one of two ways. They will either direct blame and recrimination outward toward the dominant group, or turn inward with feelings of self-blame and inferiority. This hypothesis sheds light on the negative reactions that individuals or groups who have been discriminated against sometimes exhibit toward society or themselves. It helps explain unanticipated events such as riots and revolutions.

Allport strongly suggested that prejudice is an integral part of some personality structures. He explored in some depth the prejudiced personality (referred to by some writers as the "authoritarian personality"). Weak egos unable to cope with the vicissitudes of life are, he found, susceptible to and even characterized by functional prejudice.

Admittedly there is need for refinement in terms of research into personality types. Also, there is a need for caution insofar as generic pronouncements relative to personality types are concerned.

Allan Postman collaborated with Allport in a series of studies on rumor. In one of their most famous experiments subjects were shown a picture of a roughly dressed white man holding a razor and arguing with a rather well dressed black man who had assumed a subservient posture. When asked to describe the scene, many reported erroneously, basing their perceptions on a cultural expectation. The reality of the picture was transformed, and the black man was perceived as threatening the white man. This experiment supports the contention that reality is filtered through a cultural prism—the view that not truth, but a view of truth is at the base of much human behavior. It underlines the tendency of observers to see or hear only those facts which support their beliefs and to overlook other aspects of a situation. This should alert us to potential problems in studies relying on observational techniques.

The experiment has furthered the study of rumor, for it reveals that many rumors are passed simply for the sake of interesting conversation or a different kind of story. Additional work on rumors by Allport and his colleagues centered on the how and why of rumor circulation. Allport used the term "embedding process" to describe the effort to reduce the stimulus in rumor to a simple and meaningful structure that has adaptive significance for the listener in terms of his own interests. Allport examined rumor as a catalyst for demonstrations, movements, and other types of mass behavior.

Through their analysis of the life histories of figures involved in the Nazi revolution, Allport and his colleagues have made mass movements and crowd behavior more comprehensible phenomena. They concluded, as did Durkheim, that the crowd is more than a collection of individuals, that each member is somehow different when in a crowd than when alone. Allport believed that group support encouraged the blind subservience prevalent in Nazism. The methodology of the study is well respected, since its authors gathered biographical information on over ninety Nazi leaders to arrive at their generalizations.

RUTH BENEDICT

Ruth Benedict studied anthropology under Franz Boas. She initially followed the Boasian tradition of intensive field work in a particular area, but later broke with that tradition by introducing the psychological analysis of culture into her work. In-spired by the work of Nietzsche, Spengler, and Dilthey, Benedict blended interests in German philosophy with her anthropological perspective.

Benedict's Ph.D. dissertation, written under Boas, was called "The Concept of the Guardian Spirit in North America." It traced both style and individual features of tribal-geographic variation. In Boas's historical framework, culture represented an inventory of beliefs, values, and artifacts borrowed by a group of people from a wide range of sources. Benedict's guardian spirit complex illustrated how cultural elements became separated from larger constellations and dispersed over wide areas. Tribes then selec-tively incorporated these elements into their guardian spirit complex on the basis of interests and goals.

Benedict shifted from a historical to a psychocultural model of culture in *Patterns of Culture,* an inquiry into the relation-ship between individual and culture. After studying the Dobu in Melanesia, she characterized their culture as hostile; prone to magic, witchcraft, and sorcery; and preoccupied with identifying their enemies. Outsiders would judge the Dobuans' hostile, sus-picious, jealous behavior as irrational, whereas it really repre-sented a rational reaction to their cultural environment. Culture, Benedict maintained, fashions a personality which is normal and adaptive for that society. She reached a similar conclusion after studying the Zuni of New Mexico. They, however, stressed con-formity, which gave rise to a form of social control and a differ-ent basic personality type.

Prior to publication of her classic work *Patterns of Culture,* Benedict wrote a paper on personality types among American In-dians of the Southwest and the Plains. She drew upon Nietzsche's distinction between Dionysian and Apollonian temperaments to develop a typology of culture based upon psychological types. According to Benedict, mankind has a great range of potential and purpose available to it. Individuals choose among the options available to them in order to achieve direction and meaning in their life. She credited Zuni ancestors with having set the tone for contemporary culture by favoring a temperament that fol-lowed a middle ground and avoided psychological and emotional

RUTH BENEDICT

115

excess. They represented the Apollonian style of life. In contrast to this she set the Dionysian pattern, which thrives on excitement and danger.

According to Benedict's approach, once a group's ancestors have selected a prevailing temperament, the course of development of the culture is scoured until a body of tradition and culture consistent with the temperament is developed. The result is an integrated culture that represents more than the sum of its individual traits. This integrating principle pervades all of life and gives the culture its distinctive character. Normality, then, is relative to the cultural temperament under observation, for individuals are malleable in terms of their culture. This view is also developed in the writings of Margaret Mead.

Benedict was the first to remark upon continuity in cultural conditioning, with regard to socialization generally and to sex role learning in particular. She observed that we learn skills and attitudes in one period of life which can be used later, and she documented this theory of continuity in the socialization experiences of Cheyenne Indians, showing how individuals were prepared for future adult roles through experiences in their childhood. Discontinuity, its opposite, occurs when the experiences of one life stage have little relevance in the next. In *The Chrysanthemum and the Sword,* a study of Japanese culture, Benedict called attention to the dichotomy between permissiveness and discipline in Japanese character. She associated this duality with discontinuities in childhood training. Here, her progression from a historical to a psychological anthropologist is almost complete. In a somewhat Freudian vein, Benedict stressed the importance of infantile experiences on character development.

Thanks to Benedict's research, contemporary examinations of socialization patterns can determine if we are providing continuity and whether or not what we define as continuous is actually useful. Current high rates of mental illness might indicate that we are not preparing people to cope successfully with social change.

JOHN DEWEY

Whether we are aware of it or not, the philosophy of John Dewey has touched the lives of us all. His efforts in education restructured one of America's most basic social institutions, the school. His vision of what education could become and his faith in democracy and progress combined to produce a critical reexamination of American society.

Born in Burlington, Vermont, in 1859, John Dewey graduated from the University of Vermont and began his distinguished career as a teacher in the high school of South Oil City, Pennsylvania. After deciding on a career in the teaching of philosophy, he earned a Ph.D. from Johns Hopkins University. He subsequently taught at Columbia University and at the Universities of Michigan, Minnesota, and Chicago. He founded the famous laboratory school at the University of Chicago, served as president of the American Psychological Association, and was the founder and first president of the American Association of University Professors.

Although Dewey was a philosopher and psychologist by training, he did much to advance the field of sociology—especially the sociology of education, which had roots in the writings of Emile Durkheim.

School and Society, written in 1899, was the first work to present a systematic treatment of institutional education. In this book Dewey espoused democracy as a way of life and gave the school a key role in its development. In 1916 he wrote *Democracy and Education,* a work that greatly stimulated sociological interest in education.

Dewey is generally considered to be the father of progressive education, a movement that tried to adapt the schools to changing times. Progressive, child-centered education was a reaction to earlier educational models that superimposed adult values and experiences on the child. Dewey brought to progressive education the philosophy of pragmatism, which centered everything in experience. Some progressivists rejected pragmatism and took positions far more extreme than Dewey's. His 1938 book, *Experience and Education,* sought to change classroom goals from mastery of subject matter to concern for the development of the child. He did not discount subject matter, but sought instead to define education as growth. He placed the child at the center of the curriculum and viewed the school as a function of society. Effective

JOHN DEWEY

118

teaching was measured by the child's growth and movement toward maturity.

Respect for the personality of the child was crucial to Dewey's philosophy. He did not advocate submission to the child's immediate wants and needs, but taught that the child's present and potential place in society must be considered. He was of the opinion that man ought to actively reshape his environment, and he displayed an abiding faith in social progress. Although he saw the need for the child to accept and adjust to society, he also recognized the child's right to challenge it. In Dewey's model, the school fits the child to make adjustments to society in terms of his own unique personality.

Dewey worked to improve the school, society's most important socialization arena outside the family. He reformed the school as an institution and he refined the methodological expertise of those who practice within it. Most important for sociology, he alerted the discipline to the crucial role of the school in upholding the value system of society and in shaping myriad social phenomena.

Sigmund Freud

Sigmund Freud was born in Freiberg, Moravia, now Czechoslovakia, in 1856. His family had enjoyed mild prosperity but dropped to the brink of poverty and moved to Vienna in 1870, after the collapse of the wool trade in Freiberg. His father suffered through long periods of unemployment and was not able to restore himself as a successful role model for young Freud.

In 1873 Sigmund Freud entered the University of Vienna to study medicine; he wanted to study the human condition, and during his training he engaged in biological research, coming especially under the influence of Ernst von Brücke. He joined the Vienna General Hospital in 1882 in order to gain clinical experience to eventually earn a living as a general practitioner. He continued his research, concentrating on the human brain and aspects of neurology. During this time he also investigated the therapeutic use of cocaine, research that reportedly led to personal problems with the drug. This was followed by a brief period of study under a Parisian neurologist, J. M. Charcot.

SIGMUND FREUD

Freud began to practice neuropathology in Vienna. He was first affiliated with the Kassowitz Children's Clinic, where he gathered case materials for three works on cerebral paralysis in children. He later lectured on neuropathology and psychoanalysis at the University of Vienna, opening a line of inquiry into neurological events underlying various psychological processes.

His work with Josef Breuer, culminating in *Studies in Hysteria,* provided Freud with clinical experience in psychoanalysis. Gradually, though, Freud abandoned clinical work and engaged more in theorizing on thought and behavior. His treatment of hysteria at the Kassowitz Clinic hinted at this theoretical bias. Up until that time, hysteria had been treated physically; that is, a traumatic event (psychological) was thought to combine with a physical disability (a weak nervous system) to result in hysteria. Breuer introduced Freud to a new approach. He observed that patients enjoyed temporary relief—catharsis—after describing the manifestations of their condition to him. He also recommended hypnosis to relieve patients temporarily of their symptoms. The combination of cathartic and hypnotic methods eventually resulted in the free association method. Freud believed that by studying ideas freely offered by an uncontrolled patient, the therapist could piece together clues to the patient's neurosis. In conjunction with the free association method, Freud began to form his concepts of the unconscious, repression, and transference. Ideas unacceptable in conscious thought are repressed to the unconscious, he said; they influence that which enters the conscious, but remain in the unconscious. Sociologists, of course, realize the social consequences of such phenomena.

In *Interpretation of Dreams* and *Three Essays on the Theory of Sexuality,* Freud developed the pleasure principle of discharge of excitation by psychic components. He differentiated the ego and the id and refined what he referred to as the "primary process." His double interest in psychology and neurology is seen again in his view of the sexual origins of neurosis and in his belief that dreams are wish fulfillment processes. These ideas, however, are not germane to our present concern with the sociological implications of Freud's work.

Interpretation of Dreams refines Freud's ideas on the workings of the unconscious and on its defense mechanisms, many of which have social significance. It discusses displacement, the transfer of love or hate from one person to another in order to make the emotion more acceptable to the ego, which Freud viewed as the gatekeeper of the conscious. Repressed thought and the frequent appearance in conscious thought of symbols associated therewith are also treated in this work. A socially consequential example of displacement is seen in the transfer of hate for a sibling to another person in one's environment, perhaps someone whose eyes are the same color as those of the despised sibling. Behavior thought of as deviant or delinquent might be what Freud calls "regressive behavior," or behavior equivalent to earlier thought patterns.

Freud outlined several phases of human development in his essays on the theory of sexuality. The well-known oral, anal, and phallic stages, distinguished according to sources of excitation, provide the premises for his development model. Adult behavior, he contended, was most influenced by the nature of one's passage through the successive stages of psychosexual development. Freud's theory of socialization—reflective of his view of man as savage, lustful, and quarrelsome by nature—can be deduced from this theory of development. He saw socialization as a struggle between biological impulses and culturally established norms of behavior. He traced social problems in adults to frustration in early stages of development. Regardless of his biological bias, Freud did alert us to the importance of isolating phases of human development and studying their impact upon a person throughout the life cycle. Since Freud's theories are widely employed by psychoanalysts and psychiatrists to treat problems of development, his contribution to the study of socialization must be considered here.

An implied theory of socialization is more fully drawn in *The Ego and the Id*. Here, he elaborated on the concept of the superego, described as Freud's version of a conscience; it is created, he said, by parental criticisms and prohibitions and is related to the mechanism of guilt. The superego is a helpful concept for sociologists of the family because it can be equated with parental expectation and the moralization of children. It can be viewed as a yardstick against which children measure their achievements.

Thus, the superego, roughly equivalent to the human conscience, is responsible for the differential internalization of culturally patterned behavior on the part of the child. Positive or negative parental reactions to behavior (sanctions), reflecting the broader sociocultural interpretations, converge on the child in a way that inculcates concepts of right and wrong, morality and immorality. The latter pair seems to be a function of frequently transmitting the feeling, directly or indirectly, that one "sins," not just against the expectations or desires of parents or others in society, but also against the wishes or demands of a supernatural being or beings. A practice or process from the mundane world is thus projected into the supraempirical realm. The control of children by parental actions, powerfully reinforced by concepts of the supernatural, is a relatively effective mechanism for inducing inhibitory, self-repressive tendencies.

The guilt mechanism referred to earlier functions as a powerful means of internal control which often obviates the need for formal, external, coercive social controls. Inasmuch as the inhibiting process begins quite early in life and is so intensive, the product is often thought to be innate.

Totem and Taboo is Freud's most important volume on social theory. It deals with the universal taboos against incest and against killing the totem animal, whose deification is thought to be a forerunner of religious systems. The work discusses Oedipal desire and hostility between members of society. Oedipal desire is repressed through the superego, the incorporated parental wish; it then becomes institutionalized in social justice. As in the capillarity principle of water, though, Oedipal aggression might be repressed, but desire is not. The wish must still be dealt with. The social consequences become great since the wish has power over the individual.

Some of his followers criticized Freud for his insistence on the universality of the Oedipus complex and the importance he placed upon it. Eventually, this criticism led to the Neo-Freudian movement and the study of cultural variations in personality development. Disciples of Freud who departed from specific tenets of the psychoanalytic tradition include Alfred Adler and Otto Rank. Adler departed over the Oedipus complex; Rank over Freud's insistence on the birth trauma.

Some sociologists have applied Freud's theories of development to social problems such as criminal behavior. Criminal behavior is understood as a symbolic release of repressed complexes—that is, ideas or impulses formed in early childhood are discarded by the conscious mind, but are not censored by the superego. The complexes are later expressed indirectly through criminal behavior.

In the above explanation, an inadequate superego leads to criminal behavior because it cannot control instincts; overcontrol of these drives is also thought to lead to criminal behavior. Proponents of the framework relate the resolution of the Oedipal conflict to the type of criminal behavior engaged in by the individual.

Freud's writings were enthusiastically received in America. They were welcomed by physicians, the greatest proponents of psychoanalysis, and consequently by laymen as well. On the strength of Freud's ideas, American medicine and behavioral science turned their attention to the study of early childhood development and the sexual determinants of behavior. Unfortunately, the Americans perverted his methodological traditions in that they used psychoanalysis more as a therapeutic than as a theoretical or research method.

Even though sociologists have looked to Freud's thoughts on personality to help them understand socialization, they have generally been more amenable to the Neo-Freudians, who deemphasize biological variables. Recent inquiry into the sociology of sex roles will prompt a reexamination of Freud that will challenge his belief in biological determination of social roles. Freudian interpretations and psychotherapeutic techniques are being increasingly challenged in terms of their efficaciousness.

ERICH FROMM

Erich Fromm is regarded as one of the world's leading authorities in psychoanalysis and social psychology. His writings in both fields are replete with lessons for the sociologist. He developed a unique theory of man based largely on an attempt to reconcile the theoretical frameworks of Freud and Marx. "Social character" was a major intermediate concept in this reconciliation.

Fromm was born in Frankfurt, Germany, in 1900. He received a Ph.D. in psychology from the University of Heidelberg in 1922 and completed advanced work in psychology, psychiatry, and psychoanalysis in Munich and Berlin. Fromm's background holds an important key to understanding his interests and academic pursuits. He was raised in an Orthodox German Jewish family. The family on his father's side had a long rabbinical tradition. Fromm himself was the product of talmudic teaching which encouraged the pursuit of learning and the practice of love and justice. He gave up serious religious practice while in his early twenties but incorporated the humanistic aspects of his earlier training into his value system. The experiences in Europe following World War I motivated Fromm to probe the basis of mass behavior.

Fromm favored independent inquiry into the serious topics of man, society, and the relationship of man and society. His own investigations spanned many subjects; yet his approach was always to apply his clinical experience as a psychoanalyst to the complex interrelationship of man and society. He supported the notion of social progress and assigned man an active role in determining the direction of society. He also believed in man's capacity for love and reason, the tools with which humanity would meet the challenges of survival.

Trained in the Freudian tradition, Fromm nonetheless rejected its patriarchalism. He also found Freudian techniques confining in a patient-analyst relationship. Fromm saw in the writings of Karl Marx a dynamic for understanding the process of history. He wanted to combine Marx's concept of the socioeconomic process with the biologically given conditions of human existence. His theory deals with man's need for growth and his effort to reach satisfaction in being himself. It acknowledges the sociobiological necessity for assimilation and socialization, which it substitutes for Freud's physiological dicta.

The concept of social character is basic to Fromm's theory of man, and it holds the key to his attempt to integrate psychoanalytic concepts and Marxian theory. It refers to a kind of basic per-

ERICH FROMM

sonality, a structure that Fromm believed to be internalized and shared by most members of society. Members of a society, he observed, feel satisfied when they act in accordance with its character structure.

In his book, *From Instinct to Character,* Fromm argued that processes such as aggression can be understood only by examining the conditions of existence that are specific to man because of his biological situation. He called for the study of the interaction between man's biological needs and his social conditions.

Sociologists today see relevance in Fromm's ideas on socialization. He warned that individuals will not act in conformity with a society's value system unless the society socializes them to desire these values. Contemporary sociologists also respect Fromm's analysis of the lack of attachment in society, or what he called the lack of love. They assign the modern family a pivotal role in filling this void, and their discussions of society's most basic institution often assess the role of the family in providing psychological well-being to its members.

Erich Fromm is an excellent example of an interdisciplinary theorist. The concerns he raises impinge greatly on legitimate sociological questions.

KURT LEWIN

Kurt Lewin was an esteemed social psychologist, considered by many to be the founder of the group dynamics movement in the United States. He was driven out of Germany by the Nazis. In America, he taught at Cornell University and the University of Iowa. He also founded the Research Center for Group Dynamics at the Massachusetts Institute of Technology. His work bridges the fields of social psychology and sociology.

From the notion of "social space," which has its own reality, Lewin created the conceptual scheme called field theory. It conceptualizes the impact of environment (social space) on individuals by describing their decisions and actions in terms of "locomotion" under social and psychological pressures in an environment. The scheme uses diagrams based on typological geometry to depict relationships between individuals in a field of social space.

KURT LEWIN

Field theorists address themselves to the total situation rather than to specific details. Their approach is ahistorical in that it concentrates on an individual's present field.

Lewin's skill in experimentation complemented his desire to devise designs to test his theories of group behavior. He and his colleagues cooperated in classic experiments on leadership styles; the effect of group decisions on individual behavior, such as the changing of food habits; and the initiation of social change through the creation of isolated cultural islands. Central to Lewin's experiments on the introduction of social change was the notion of a "gatekeeper," identified as an influential primary group member who monitors the entrance of outsiders and outside ideologies into the group. The gatekeeper's function parallels that of the ego in the Freudian framework.

Lewin's thoughts on the emancipation of the Jew are relevant for the sociological study of race and ethnic minorities. He pointed out that Jews, because of the subdivided nature of their group, have unique identity problems. They are subject to conflict, especially if their religious, social, and other roles are not compatible. Jews and other minorities who find security in group membership within their ethnic or racial ghettos often experience anomie and a sense of homelessness when they enter larger social worlds. Lewin recommended a strong, positive identity as their most forceful weapon against anger, self-pity, and hostility. It emerges, he said, when these feelings are discussed as a social issue rather than an individual problem.

Bronislaw Malinowski

Born in Kráków, Poland, in 1884, Bronislaw Malinowski—a social anthropologist—added to both the ethnographic and methodological treasuries of the social sciences. His early formal training was in physics and mathematics, but he became interested in anthropology after reading Fraser's *Golden Bough*. He studied at Leipzig under William Wundt and Karl Buecher, and in London under such scholars as L. T. Hobhouse, Edward A. Westermarck, and C. G. Seligman. Seligman acted as Malinowski's adviser and encouraged his entry into field work.

BRONISLAW MALINOWSKI

The bulk of Malinowski's academic career was spent at the London School of Economics, where he served as the first chairman of the social anthropology department. He conducted field work on a number of exotic peoples and places, including the Motu in Papula, the Mailu of New Guinea, and the Trobriand Islanders.

Malinowski is a pivotal figure in the evolution of anthropological and hence social scientific methodology. His field methods and his dedication to field work revolutionized anthropology. He was a pioneer in what we now refer to as participant observation, a method taken for granted by younger sociologists and anthropologists. The anthropologist can no longer be content to remain at the university desk philosophizing about the life of exotic peoples on the basis of reports being brought back by missionaries or world travelers. Among Malinowski's field monographs are: *Argonauts of the Western Pacific* (1922), *Sexual Life of Savages* (1929), and *Coral Gardens and their Magic* (1935).

Along with Radcliffe-Brown, Malinowski argued against the type of historical reconstruction fashionable in early twentieth-century anthropology. His own work, which he termed "functional anthropology," illustrated that customs or cultural traits always have a function in the larger cultural system; they are not simply remnants of an earlier tradition. He described several specific activities among Trobriand Islanders, but each was a coordinated part of an institution governed by broader societal rules. Detailed charts helped him correlate the major activities of the people described here and in other studies. His data-gathering methods were based on his perception of what he called "cultural imperatives"—the essential aspects of a culture.

Malinowski did not accept the prevailing evolutionary or diffusion theories; he relied instead on straightforward description and careful analysis of individuals and traits as part of a total cultural system. His field accounts reflect the breadth of his knowledge, for they offer original insights into such diverse problems as family organization, primitive law, kinship terminology, magic, religion, myth, and linguistics. Malinowski's strong academic stands and colorful personality are said to have provoked much turmoil in the field.

MARGARET MEAD

Born in Philadelphia, Pennsylvania, in 1901, Margaret Mead received a Ph.D. in anthropology from Columbia University. She enjoyed a distinguished career with the American Museum of Natural History and with various academic centers. Although Mead at first patterned her work after that of Franz Boas, her interest in psychological aspects of culture moved her away from some traditional anthropological concerns. Her numerous descriptive accounts of other cultures are models of culture-free theorizing and contain a storehouse of information on social processes, personality and mental health, national character, and social change and development.

Many of her early works have gone through at least three revisions. Among her most famous studies are *Coming of Age in Samoa; New Lives for Old: Cultural Transformation, Sex and Temperament in Three Primitive Societies;* and *Male and Female.* The last-named work has received renewed recognition in the 1970s due to changes in the status and role of women in American society. Her description of the Kwakiutl in *Cooperation and Conflict among Primitive Peoples,* another highly regarded work, demonstrates that no society is exclusively competitive or cooperative.

Mead is perhaps best known to sociologists for her theories on cultural and social change. Her accounts discuss the structural aspects of change in society and the influence of culture change on personality development. The Palauans of Micronesia, whose culture she describes in *Cultural Patterns and Technological Change,* illustrate that native peoples are not always demoralized by contact with other cultures. These peoples preserved traditional culture and blended it with the new Western commercialism. Mead disagreed with the idea that slow culture change is best for native peoples. Rapid change, because it does not allow the accumulation of cultural lags over time, may, she felt, be less disturbing than slow, selective change. Her study of cultural change among the Manus supported this argument.

Mead became not only one of the most honored social scientists of recent times, but also a renowned lecturer on popular culture.

MARGARET MEAD

133

She became a kind of folk hero to the activist students of the 1960s. Her cross-cultural studies supplied her with data on sex roles and practices in various societies, so the changes advocated by the American young did not always seem unreasonable to her. She felt that the generation gap could be spanned only if parents were willing to reverse roles and sit at the feet of their children.

Sociologists share with anthropologists a deep interest in the concept of culture. Margaret Mead did much to bridge these two sciences.

Margaret Mead died in November 1978. In the view of many professionals (and laymen as well), anthropology has lost its preeminent figure.

ROBERT MICHELS

Political Parties, Robert Michels's study of socialist and trade union organizations in Europe during the early part of the twentieth century, noted a tendency toward oligarchy in large organizations. Called "the iron law of oligarchy," the tendency has since become an important variable in research on large organizations and on forms of authority in society.

Michels saw oligarchy as inherent in organization. It increases, he said, as officials learn their roles and begin to experience power concomitant with their offices. Several researchers have examined organizations in light of Michels's theorem and have concluded that apathy among rank and file organization members fosters oligarchy among organization leaders. *Union Democracy,* a study by Lipset, Trow, and Coleman, utilized Michels's framework to ascertain conditions under which oligarchy does not occur in the organizational context. The iron law of oligarchy interests sociologists because human organization is a central concept within the discipline, and leadership is generally considered a necessary component of organization. Furthermore, Michels's theory directly addresses power relationships and their influence on organizational operations.

Michels's work has been superseded by studies which indicate that it is possible for large organizations to operate democratically by being less rational and more informal than Michels felt possible. Nevertheless, his work did alert us to a lurking danger in the operation of organizations as well as to a potential source of conflict in society.

GEORGE P. MURDOCK

George P. Murdock is one of the most distinguished modern anthropologists. He has taught at Yale, the University of Pittsburgh, and elsewhere and has served as president of both the Society for Applied Anthropology and the American Ethnological Society.

Murdock's intellectual pursuits are of special significance to the sociologist because they center on questions of social organization and social structure. His approach to knowledge is systematic and formal, and he has sought to utilize knowledge irrespective of the discipline from which it derives. His book *Social Structure* draws on various sciences for interpretations of the institution of kinship. It utilizes data on 250 societies in a discussion of variations in kinship structures. Murdock seeks a degree of regularity and conformity in social organization similar to the levels postulated in the natural sciences.

Much of Murdock's work is a search for cultural uniformities or universals, such as the nuclear family. He approached these universals through a combination of statistical-correlational checks and historical evaluation. He pursued the search for cultural universals first through the Yale Cross Cultural Survey and then via the Human Relations Area Files, the latter being a pragmatic classification device that details the ways in which social scientists and others organize their materials. It is the result of joint university, foundation, and governmental activity aimed at assembling, translating, classifying, and at reproducing in accessible form the descriptive materials of anthropologists. This system approaches classification schemes used in the natural sciences. Without the type of codification advocated by Murdock, the social sciences cannot hope to gain acceptance as true sciences.

GUNNAR MYRDAL

As a Swedish social economist at the University of Stockholm, Gunnar Myrdal was brought to the United States by the Carnegie Corporation to undertake a neutral study of race in America.

GEORGE P. MURDOCK

136

When his two-volume report, *An American Dilemma,* first appeared in 1944, it altered American attitudes toward race relations. Its impact on the organization of social research in this country was even greater, though, for it was one of the first heavily financed and highly institutionalized research studies in the social sciences.

The report did not represent a breakthrough in terms of substantive materials, but it organized existing facts and information in such a way as to promote public understanding of race and race-related problems. Myrdal treated the racial problem as a moral issue and as a challenge to the American people. He framed it as a conflict between the American creed, with its general supporting value system, and the individual value systems of citizens and local interest groups. The problem then became one of attempting to reconcile these two levels of conflicting values. Myrdal advised that racial issues in America be treated as part of the existing societal value system and not in the abstract.

The research reported in *An American Dilemma* described the social, political, educational, and economic status of the American black. It also detailed attitudes of both whites and blacks as to the status of blacks in the United States. The study documented changes in the status of blacks and examined the institutional and other mechanisms leading to these changes. Myrdal summarized the character of American race relations in terms of what he called the "rank order of discrimination," a ranking of racial concerns among the white population.

Methodologically, *An American Dilemma* contains a number of lessons for both the novice and the seasoned sociologist. Foremost among these lessons is the way in which Myrdal dealt with his own values relative to race. Before undertaking his investigation, he inventoried himself, to set forth his own feelings about race. This inventory would allow readers to reflect on the interplay between the researcher's values and his findings. It is good advice for all researchers to follow when they begin their own investigations. The study made extensive use of documents, observation, interviews, and other techniques. It was well planned and utilized the expertise of a large number of social scientists, many of them excellent sociologists.

Myrdal's approach was guided by the thinking of sociologist W. I. Thomas. He followed Thomas's theorem that situations defined as real are real in their consequences and employed his concept of the definition of the situation.

An American Dilemma is indeed a hallmark—in the precedent it set for the conduct and organization of social research and in the signal it sounded for sociology's involvement in public policy. It has also been a consciousness-raising device for many Americans.

ROBERT REDFIELD

A consistent contributor to the development of ethnology within anthropology, Robert Redfield was a distinguished professor of anthropology at the University of Chicago. Much of his work centered on the meaning of values in traditional folk communities and the impact of urbanization on community values and social change. He drew attention to the place of community studies in the social sciences.

Redfield's *Tepoztlan: A Mexican Village*, written in 1930, was the first ethnological study of the meaning of values in the life of a traditional Mexican village. It represented the beginning of general research on a rural-urban continuum of communities on the Yucatán Peninsula. It was also the basis for Redfield's conceptualization of the folk society and for his analysis of change as a result of urbanization. The folk society represented an ideal model based on a relatively isolated, self-sufficient, and ceremonious community. It accented group as opposed to individual interests; kinship, custom, and tradition; and the moral order. The folk society construct stressed common social experiences and bonds of identity. It saw this cohesion being disrupted by technological and other changes associated with urbanism.

In *The Folk Culture of Yucatán* Redfield developed a classic explication of the concept of acculturation. He described the process by which the sacred customs of the folk society were secularized by emerging urban trends.

The structuralist influences of the sociologist Durkheim and the anthropologist Radcliffe-Brown are apparent in Redfield's beliefs about the ritualization of custom. He also subscribed to develop-

ROBERT REDFIELD

139

mental models that perceived societies as moving from the sacred to the secular, from the homogeneous to the heterogeneous, and from ethically less advanced to ethically more advanced states. Redfield felt that there was an absolute human ethic toward which mankind directed its expression, the highest aspect of which could be found in the moral commitments of civilized communities. His focus on value orientations as germane to cultural integration coincided with dominant anthropological perspectives, but he diverged from others in the field by calling attention to psychological variables. Members of society shared an organized mental life, he said, and they applied it to the resolution of their common problems. In contrasting urban and rural villages in Yucatán, Redfield uncovered value differences arising from the integrated moral universe of the rural society as opposed to the heterogeneous secular universe of the urban. He maintained that an examination of value premises would shed light on cultural differences.

Redfield's two volumes on Chan Kom—*Chan Kom, a Maya Village* and *A Village That Chose Progress*—contain ethnographic materials on the effects of economic and political change on developing communities. He first visited Chan Kom around 1930, when it was a folk society in transition. When he revisited it in 1948, he was impressed with the way in which the villagers had adapted to change. They harmonized tradition and change. Redfield felt that Chan Kom successfully adjusted to change because it had the ideological and moral foundations that modernization required. Many of his accounts of folk societies point up the need to examine the ideology and world view of the people being studied.

Despite his fascination with folk societies, Redfield did not engage in description as an end in itself. *Peasant Society and Culture* suggests ways in which anthropologists and other social scientists can approach the study of complex societies through the study of more primitive ones.

Since the concepts of community and social and cultural change are integral to sociology as well as to anthropology, the work of Redfield continues to enjoy visibility in both fields. Many so-

ciologists today lament the corruption of the term "community."
Redfield's work is a reminder of the place of this term in our
scientific legacy.

THOMAS S. SZASZ

Thomas Szasz was born in Budapest in 1920. He received both
A.B. and M.D. degrees from the University of Cincinnati, the
latter in 1944. He was trained in psychiatry at the University of
Chicago and obtained his psychoanalytic preparation at the Chicago Institute for Psychoanalysis. Dr. Szasz is a member of the
American Psychoanalytic Association and a fellow of the American Psychiatric Association. Reflecting one of his major interests,
Szasz is a cofounder and chairman of the board of the American
Association for the Abolition of Involuntary Mental Hospitalization. Currently, he is a professor of psychiatry at the State University of New York Upstate Medical Center in Syracuse.

Szasz is not a sociologist. His inclusion in this volume is based
on the assumption that an important function of the sociologist
is to question conventional wisdom, from the standpoint of either
empirical research or imaginative creative insights. Dr. Szasz
indubitably qualifies on that count. He has seriously challenged
many accepted theories about modern psychiatry, social psychology, and society generally.

In writing about the negative political and social ramifications of
institutional psychiatry, Szasz understandably has not endeared
himself to many in his profession. He has gained a reputation for
radical thought. Be that as it may, his contention that the concept
of mental illness is erroneous, and thus misleading, is worthy of
serious consideration. He elaborated on this subject in *The Myth
of Mental Illness,* published in 1961. The work argues that the
term "mental illness" is a misleading metaphor with serious social
consequences, such as the use of force, fraud, and long-term
incarceration. It legitimizes inhumanity and supports authoritarianism.

Dr. Szasz makes a distinction between what are called mental
illnesses and psychiatric disorders. Toxic psychosis, for example,
is considered a disease of the brain, not the mind. He also clearly
distinguishes between mental illness and forms of social deviation

such as homosexuality. The American Psychiatric Association no longer considers homosexuality as a mental illness. Thus, Szasz recognizes the definitional aspect of behavior and, as Ruth Benedict did in *Patterns of Culture,* the temporal aspect in terms of what appears in psychiatric manuals.

In *Manufacture of Madness,* published in 1970, he analyzes the mental health movement as a tool used to enforce social conformity. He looks upon the group, or society, as a function of a uniformity of common ideas and values. Questioning or rejecting such commonality has come to be viewed as dysfunctional or potentially destructive. In the interest of solidarity, institutional psychiatry inhibits independent thought, thus reinforcing a dominant ethic. Szasz fears the power of the psychiatrist to condemn the social heretic. Another of his works, *Psychiatric Justice,* presents case histories illustrating the plight of the individual who is confronted with the charge of mental illness and denied, without trial, his civil liberties—a powerful indictment of the judicial process.

Dr. Szasz is one of the most pungent, iconoclastic, libertarian, and original critics of psychiatry. His discussions of the social problems inherent in the relationship between the mental health movement and the social order locate him, at least peripherally, within the province of sociology. Viewed within a frame of reference involving sociological and cross-cultural anthropological data, Szasz's work could conceivably generate an eclectic theory relative to social variance and social control.

THORSTEIN VEBLEN

Thorstein Veblen was born in Wisconsin in 1857. He was educated at Johns Hopkins, Yale, and Cornell Universities. Of his writings, *The Theory of the Leisure Class* has received the most attention. Here he first used the now famous phrase "conspicuous consumption" to suggest that people buy and use goods visibly to indicate or lay claim to a social position. He observed that people often estimate the social class of another by evaluating his visible possessions.

Veblen also proposed a broader theory of society. He tried to demonstrate that social relations and culture are shaped by tech-

THORSTEIN VEBLEN

143

nology. He studied the habits that grow out of the opportunities for expression contained in the material environment and from his inquiry formulated an evolutionary view that depicted society as a process of man's mental adaptation to circumstances which no longer tolerate existing habits. Change, he said, is a slow process, facilitated mainly by the exposure of individuals to the constraining forces of the environment. Social groups such as class groupings, which are sheltered from the total environment, will change more slowly and hence retard the transformation of the total society. For Veblen, the leisure class was one such element.

He advanced a theory of class conflict that was rooted in technological conditions. William Ogburn's concept of culture lag mirrors Veblen's conception of technology as an instrument of social change. His most lasting mark on modern sociology seems to have been made not by his evolutionary framework, but by his description of both the leisure class and the imitation thereof by the remainder of society.

Veblen enriched our descriptive vocabulary; and his thought, clothed in such verbal adornments as "trained incapacity," "predatory culture," "absentee ownership," and "conspicuous consumption," continues to condition our view of economic and social reality. In fact, whether or not we attribute them to him, such terms have become part of popular parlance.

Veblen's analyses were only precariously buttressed by empirical data. With the possible exception of *The Higher Learning in America: A Memorandum on the Conduct of Universities by Businessmen,* a 1918 work involving participant observation, his methodology was impressionistic. Many students are unfamiliar with his work, for he is not widely read. However one might react to his techniques and approaches to reality (and some automatically discount the products of impressionism), this impressionistic-interpretive sociologist has had a lasting and forceful impact on socioeconomic thought.

Chapter 5

Contemporary Contributors

In the introduction to this volume, the science of sociology was referred to as a systematic study of the social order. The authors noted the critical nature of the quest for knowledge in the modern era, an era threatened by persistent social problems. Previous sections focused on the founders of the discipline and on those who added new dimensions to it and to the search for truth. Their dedication to humanitarian concerns has enhanced our understanding of the human condition. With appreciation and a sense of indebtedness, the authors briefly reviewed the products of their skill, imagination, and intellectual labor.

The final section points up the work of individuals who have fostered the growth and maturation of the present-day sociological perspective. Although all have enriched the discipline and have earned a sterling reputation for intellectual achievements, it is difficult to assess their overall impact on the field inasmuch as most are still building their legacy.

The introduction to the first section of this work remarked upon the diverse origins of sociology. That diversity continues to characterize the field, as evidenced by the individuals discussed in this final section. Some have explored broad societal questions, while others have found sociology to be more useful on a specific microcosmic level. They have approached the discipline from a variety of perspectives—order, conflict, symbolic interactionism, structural functionalism, and the eclectic.

145

Sociology as a discipline has enjoyed remarkable growth and acceptance over the past few decades. The number of scientists calling themselves sociologists has increased dramatically, a trend reflected in this section's discussions of twenty-one individual sociologists. As was the case in previous sections, it is impossible to do justice to all who might be legitimately included as a result of their insights or scientific findings. To impress the reader with the broad range of topics that contemporary sociologists study, the authors have included investigators on topics as diverse as the family and deviance. Similarly, the methodologies discussed range from participant observation to social surveys to mathematical sociological techniques.

There is no study more exacting and more exciting than the study of man in society. Any of the individuals profiled herein might well serve as a model for those who are intellectually curious or who seek a more adequate view of reality in the social realm. To make their original works a part of one's intellectual experience is to be automatically enriched in terms of human understanding.

HOWARD S. BECKER

Born in Chicago, Illinois, in 1928, Howard S. Becker did his graduate work in sociology at the University of Chicago. He later taught there and at Stanford and Northwestern Universities. He has also served as editor of the journal *Social Problems*. The discipline as a whole has benefited from his work in social psychology and deviant behavior.

Becker's work is regarded for its methodology as well as its substance. In particular, he has made extensive use of the technique of observation, has pursued the use of life history documents in deviant case analysis, and has pioneered use of the case study method for purposes of gaining a holistic understanding of the phenomenon under investigation.

The process of socialization received attention in Becker's collaborative work with Blanche Geer on idealism among medical students and in his descriptive accounts of the process of becoming a marijuana user. Becker, a former musician himself, did a participant observation study of marijuana use among musicians.

He adopted a developmental approach to the problem, operating on the premise that users first enter an experience and then acquire motivations and explanations for their behavior. Becker's investigation of marijuana use follows the hypothesis that in order to continue in marijuana use one must define his initial experiences with the drug as pleasurable. This idea accords with the symbolic interactionist belief that behavior develops as a result of one's ability to interpret events, not as a result of previously existing idiosyncratic traits. This perspective, as developed by George Herbert Mead, asserts that individuals can learn new definitions of situations; hence its emphasis on socialization and relearning.

Outsiders and *The Other Side* contain Becker's most lucid applications of his interpretation of deviance. The latter volume is a collection of essays on a variety of deviant behaviors. The essays all contain the theme that deviance does not reside in behavior, but in the interaction between the person who commits an act and those who respond to it. All the essays employ the labeling perspective to explain deviance.

Labeling theory views deviance from the point of view of the individual who is labeled. Becker contends that once a person is labeled as deviant, he may then decide to cultivate that life style. An individual who is officially branded as a criminal may, for example, then begin to act like one. The labeling process leads the person who is labeled to isolate himself from situations that contain pressures toward conformity. Advocates of the perspective contend that a vicious circle ensues in which the labeled individual becomes more dependent on deviant ties for his social survival and more inclined to reorganize his life around deviant activity.

The labeling perspective is undergoing crucial reexamination in current sociology. Regardless of the outcome, Becker's descriptive and ethnographic work will continue to be read by sociologists in the years ahead.

DANIEL BELL

Daniel Bell is a political sociologist who received his Ph.D. from Columbia University in 1960. He has taught at the University of Chicago and at Columbia and Harvard Universities. Much of his

DANIEL BELL

writing deals with the quality of life in contemporary America and with trends in social change.

Bell's view of American society is far less pessimistic than that of many other leading analysts of social structure. He does not believe that the case for a ruling elite with a monopoly on power has been made for American society. In *The Coming of Post-Industrial Society* Bell forecasts long-term general patterns of change in society. He discusses new forms of interaction that he says arise to replace outmoded and ineffective forms. As an example of an effective new form of interaction, Bell offers the local trade union, where leaders are recruited from the rank and file. He interprets the high degree of voluntary association in America as an attempt to fill a void left by a lack of real sources of psychological and social satisfaction. Despite increased bureaucratization in society, the quality of life in contemporary society is, in Bell's opinion, an improvement over what it was in previous times. He believes that a new level of humanism pervades modern America.

Bell implies that the sociologist should engage in prediction and social forecasting. He asserts that sociologists have valuable input to offer to policy makers. Sociologists should, he claims, engage in objective analysis of the sociological aspects of social change. He is particularly concerned that individuals be prepared to adjust to social change without a forced sacrificing of their freedoms.

It is too soon to tell whether Bell's forecasts for postindustrial society will come to pass, although some of the trends he pinpoints seem to be correct: expansion of the service economy; an increase in middle-class and white-collar workers; further geographic separation of individuals and families; and increased dependence on computers. Other forecasts, such as the rise of the intellectuals or increased government dominance over business, seem less obvious. The new emphasis in sociology on social indicators as empirical descriptions of the state of society and the quality of life is related to Bell's perspective and interests.

In addition to the above, Bell's discussion of ideology in mid-twentieth-century America and the fragmentation of earlier rigid belief systems should be read by students interested in the sociology of knowledge and in political sociology.

PETER BERGER

Peter Berger received his Ph.D. in sociology from the New School for Social Research in 1954 and is currently a professor at Rutgers University. He has advanced general sociological theory as well as the subfields of the sociology of knowledge and the sociology of religion.

Students who are thinking about a career in sociology would do well to read Berger's *Invitation to Sociology* (1963), a nontechnical introduction to the sociological perspective. It presents an overview of the field and, more importantly, it communicates the kind of inquisitive, critical thinking that has helped sociology become a recognized discipline.

In *The Social Construction of Reality* Berger presents a unique approach to the sociology of knowledge. He argues that ideas and ideology constitute only one of its aspects. Unlike Mannheim, he denies a central role to ideology, maintaining instead that the sociology of knowledge must be concerned with everything that passes for knowledge. Berger's schema recognizes the interdependence between common sense knowledge and the construction of social reality.

The bankruptcy of modernity is a theme that Berger has explored in both his collaborative work, *The Homeless Mind,* and his recent book on the sociology of religion, *Pyramids of Sacrifice: Political Ethics and Social Change.* Because he feels that capitalism has not succeeded in creating a sense of home or purpose, he sees an increase in individual anomie in modern society and an increase in false myths which have captured collectivities.

Berger has been in the forefront of the movement to carry the framework of the sociology of religion into new areas such as the investigation of value systems. In *Pyramids of Sacrifice* he applies methods developed in his sociology of religion to an objective examination of social issues. Sociology is used as a debunking process to force the social scientist into an examination of unacknowledged myths and questions of value. He adopts a humanistic perspective and urges scientists, policymakers, and ideological trendsetters to examine the power inherent in their roles as producers and implementers of ideas. They must consider those who consume knowledge, those who can easily become entrapped by intellectual interpretations.

The role of myth as a sustaining force in society is a central theorem in Berger's recent work. He encourages us to respect the myths of others by pointing out that our modern mythology is only one explanation of social reality. Somewhat in the tradition of George Herbert Mead, Berger has forced sociology to consider the relevance of language in understanding social reality.

In a sense, Berger seems to have created a sociology of sociology. His so-called debunking process often strikes very sensitive nerves in the life system of the discipline. Without these periodic self-examinations, no discipline can expect to survive.

PETER M. BLAU

An astute student of social structure and social organization, Peter Blau was born in Vienna, Austria. He received a Ph.D. from Columbia University, where he now serves as professor of sociology. He was president of the American Sociological Association in 1973 and previously served as editor of the *American Journal of Sociology*. His research probed structure and differentiation within formal organizations and bureaucracies; social exchange and power; and occupational structure and mobility.

The *Dynamics of Bureaucracy* contains practical insights into administrative structure. In this volume, Blau demonstrates how change can come about in bureaucracies through both internal tension and cohesion. Using data drawn from observation of a particular governmental agency, he shows how attributes that were formally intended to be functional are actually dysfunctional. Together with Richard Scott he constructed a typology of organizations based on the question of cui bono ("who benefits?"). The typology has helped empirical investigators who are studying commonalities among classes of organizations. In defining formal organizations on the basis of deliberate arrangement to attain specific goals, Blau and Scott draw attention to organizational-environmental relationships: to how outside expectations mold individual performance within organizational structures and to cross-societal variation in organizational models. The distinction

PETER M. BLAU

152

between formal and informal organization is recognized throughout Blau's work. Following his lead, much contemporary research seeks answers to questions about the nature and emergence of informal organization.

In *Exchange and Power in Social Life* Blau again develops a Weberian theme. In this case, he discusses how differences, between formal and substantive rationality affect the relationship of individuals in society. Exchange relationships—those based on factors other than monetary or status gain—are important to Blau, who suggests that relationships built on such factors as gratitude are more significant than most theorists will admit. He analyzes the legitimization of authority in society, devoting most of his thought to the informal ways of enforcing or perpetuating impersonal mechanisms of authority.

Blau's perceptive development of unanswered questions in the Weberian model and his analysis of empirical cases in light of his own theoretical generalizations have combined to make him a compelling figure in the study of social organization and social structure.

JAMES S. COLEMAN

A respected name in the sociology of education, James Coleman received a Ph.D. in sociology from Columbia University in 1955. He is now a professor of sociology at the University of Chicago. In addition to his work in educational sociology, Coleman has furthered the development of mathematical sociology and the study of collective decision making and social choice.

Equality of Educational Opportunity, better known as the "Coleman Report," is a landmark volume in the involvement of sociology with public policy. The now controversial research in this book and the author's subsequent testimonies and reports have been instrumental in shaping the federal government's programs for racial integration. The decision to implement school busing, for example, arose from Coleman's recommendations. His original report was a survey of educational opportunities for children in a sample of four thousand schools. Although the study included both black and white students, it looked most closely at opportunities available to minority students and at their subsequent educational achievements. Coleman hypothesized that a child's self-concept and expectation of academic success would improve his academic performance; that is, if a child believes his efforts will make a difference in terms of his life chances, he will be more highly motivated to achieve. Coleman deemphasizes the role of teacher abilities and a school's physical plant in the educational achievement of students, particularly minority students. *Adolescent Society,* another work of Coleman's on educational sociology, identifies significant variables in the youth culture and validates the role of peer groups in the overall socialization process.

Coleman adopted a rather unique perspective on the functional nature of conflict in communities. It can break down polarization and extremism, he claimed, because it demands that issues be brought into the open and examined. The issues themselves might differ, but the process of conflict remains the same in each case. This view of conflict has been instrumental to the social work method of community organization and to the formation of groups to deal with community conflict. In a general way, Coleman's work has illuminated the concept of community and the sources of community disorganization and conflict.

LEWIS A. COSER

Lewis Coser was born in Berlin, Germany, in 1913. He received a Ph.D. from Columbia University in 1954 and has taught at several major universities, including the State University of New York at Stony Brook, where he is currently a Distinguished Professor of Sociology. In 1967 he was elected president of the Society for the Study of Social Problems, and in 1974 he became president of the American Sociological Association.

Coser's contributions to sociology have been many and varied. His published works have focused on the development of sociological theory, on social conflict, and on issues related to the analysis of social structure. His view of society as a collection of conflicting groups is very much in the Marxian tradition, while his analyses of social conflict and deviant behavior exhibit a functionalist perspective.

In *The Functions of Social Conflict,* Coser analyzes how conflict promotes social unity. It provides an opportunity to readjust the social structure by allowing for the direct expression of dissatisfaction. The problems underlying the dissatisfaction can then be dealt with. On the whole, he sees the institutionalization of conflict as a stabilizing element in society, an idea that has led sociologists to reevaluate existing concepts of social conflict. Coser's interest in conflict creates a continuity in his work. He translated Georg Simmel's ideas about conflict and social structure and has written on factors involved in establishing societal and organizational commitment.

Coser continues to enrich sociology by examining the life and work of major theorists. He is attentive to the role of ideas in the development of the discipline.

DONALD G. CRESSEY

Donald Cressey received his Ph.D. in sociology from Indiana University, a school where the study of criminal behavior has long been an integral part of the sociology program. He is currently on the faculty of the University of California at Santa Barbara. He has also been a consultant to important commissions on organized crime and criminal justice.

Cressey's work has helped to stimulate research in criminology. It shifts away from explanations of individual criminality to the study of the organization of criminal activity. Pursuing Edwin H. Sutherland's line of inquiry, Cressey has investigated crimes committed by persons during the normal course of their work— white-collar crimes. Cressey collaborated with Sutherland, his mentor, in revision of the latter's famous work *Principles of Criminology*.

The differential association theory, an explanation of criminal behavior first developed by Sutherland, provided a foundation for much of Cressey's work and he has since become its leading analyst. Cressey admits that the framework does not fit certain types of crime, such as the violation of financial trust or embezzlement; yet he feels that Sutherland has been grossly misinterpreted. Critics of Sutherland, he argues, have failed to acknowledge that the explanation applies to anticriminal as well as criminal behavior. Furthermore, he contends that Sutherland believed motiva-

DONALD G. CRESSEY

tions and rationalizations for crime as well as techniques of crime could be learned through differential association.

Other People's Money, Cressey's famous book on the social psychology of embezzlement, is based on his interviews with financial trust violators imprisoned in at least three penitentiaries, including Joliet in Illinois. His explanation rests upon the fact that the violator has a non-shareable financial problem. Cressey also discusses the rationalization that precedes the decision to violate a trust. This idea is somewhat parallel to what some scholars of delinquency and deviance refer to as "techniques of neutralization."

It should be noted that Cressey does not engage in description as an end in itself. He very carefully searches for theoretical and conceptual links between his observation and description and the ongoing sociological enterprise. An excellent example of such an attempt is found in *Theft of the Nation.* In this work he draws parallels between organized crime and the changing structure of society, contending that the former exists to provide illicit goods and services demanded by legitimate society. The real threat to society is not the individual hoodlum but the groups (he uses the term "families") who corrupt legitimate business and infiltrate governmental operations.

Although thought by some to be in a limited area of sociology, Cressey's contributions have enlarged the sociological perspective.

RALF DAHRENDORF

Ralf Dahrendorf is a conflict theorist who built his conception of society upon the Marxian tradition and his own observations in Nazi Germany. He departed from the Marxian emphasis upon social class and turned instead to political factors, especially authority relations, as the main explanatory variable for understanding society. Because his theories are derived from his own life experiences and observations, an analysis of them would illustrate the perspective adopted in the sociology of knowledge.

In *Class and Class Conflict in Industrial Society* Dahrendorf adopts the position that conflct is functional for society inasmuch as it can promote social change. His rather simplistic explanation of conflict looks at the way in which authority promotes the per-

RALF DAHRENDORF

sonal needs and rewards of the person who possesses it. Whereas Marx saw economic factors leading to conflict between the haves and the have-nots, Dahrendorf isolates ·authority relations as a source of conflict between those who have authority and want to maintain it and those who do not possess it but would like to. Dahrendorf believes that social classes can be broken down into smaller interest or conflict groups that cut across all· aspects of the social structure characterized by authority.

Like Marx, Dahrendorf offers primarily a one-variable explanation of the nature of social life; and like Marx, he does not deny that other variables can influence social structure. Dahrendorf, though, selects authority relations as the principal explanatory variable.

Amitai W. Etzioni

From the mid-1960s to the present Amitai Etzioni has been one of the most prolific spokesmen for sociology and its potential. Born in Cologne, Germany, in 1929, Etzioni has held faculty positions at Hebrew University, the University of California at Berkeley, and at Columbia University. At present he is director of the Center for Policy Research at Columbia. He has illuminated diverse areas of sociology through his study of complex organizations, his peace research, his analysis of social change and development, and his efforts for social reform.

Etzioni is a major analyst of social policy implications in the late twentieth century. Many of his later works raise future-oriented questions. In *The Active Society,* for example, he proposes a new model of an ideal society. Setting the tone for his personal involvement in social reform, he argues that a society can guide social change to achieve humane social goals. This guidance comes through the mobilization of publics who organize to work for change in accord with their interests. His futurist orientations are continued in *Genetic Fix,* where he presents a sociological analysis of issues involved in genetic counseling. He has actively debated the positive and negative aspects of genetic intervention.

In addition to his policy research and profound interest in the sources and consequences of social change, Etzioni has provided direction for a line of investigation into the workings of large bureaucratic and complex organizations. His theory of organization is closer to that of Theodore Caplow or Talcott Parsons, who see it as a social system, than it is to Max Weber's, which examines organizations in terms of social relationships. In *Modern Organizations* Etzioni supports Parsons's definition of organization by placing emphasis on goal specificity. He also suggests that organizations differ from other social units in the degree that they are in control of their nature and destiny. Organizations seem to him more consciously planned and structured than other societal units. He suggests three defining criteria of organizations: division of labor, power, and communication. To summarize his view: (1) the responsibilities of personnel are consciously planned with a view toward goal realization; (2) one or more power centers direct the organization toward goals; and (3) a concern with personnel is reflected in reallocation of tasks among members, recruitment of new members, and removal of members no longer desired.

In his *Comparative Analysis of Complex Organizations* he cross-classifies analytical concepts to construct new descriptive categories. He crosses the concept of power with the concept of involvement to form a new concept of "compliance relationship." The aim of the typology is to make systematic comparisons between classes of organizations and to construct from the data theories of the "middle range," or on a workable level, rather than in a complete societal context. Etzioni's classificatory scheme has generated many empirical studies of organization and has been a starting point for testing the interrelationship of group and individual levels within the organization. His concern with the relationship between a superior's power to control subordinates and the subordinates' orientation to this power follows traditional sociological concerns rooted in the writings of Parsons and Weber.

The three types of power differentiated by Etzioni according to the means used to make the subjects comply are: coercive, remunerative, and normative. They are concerned with physical force and restriction, control of material resources and rewards, and symbolic rewards, respectively. The three types of involvement—alienative, calculative, and moral—represent increasing degrees of

AMITAI W. ETZIONI

161

commitment on the part of members. In his cross-classification of power and involvement, which yielded nine types of compliance relationships, Etzioni saw the coercive-alienative, remunerative-calculative, and normative-moral groupings as most advantageous to an organization. These three he referred to as congruent. He called these three congruent types coercive, utilitarian, and normative. The first is exemplified by prisons and mental hospitals; the second by business and industry; the third by churches, colleges, and voluntary associations. Etzioni concluded that the other six types of organizations tended to develop towards one of the congruent types, either by changing the basis of involvement or the type of power which predominates.

Etzioni's classification then has a distinctive concern with power, a sociological variable, and involvement, a psychological variable. It moves from the study of a single organization to abstractions about classes and eventually all organizations. In fact, all of Etzioni's work is characterized by a steady building toward middle-range explanations of societal phenomena. He will be remembered both for his substantive contributions to the field of sociology and for his active commitment to social reform.

Etzioni's concern with social problems is evident not just in his scholarly publications, which exert only a mild influence, but also in numerous articles appearing in journals and periodicals. He is certainly one of the better-known modern sociologists.

HERBERT GANS

Herbert Gans is another leading American sociologist who was born in Germany. Unlike most sociologists, Gans has taken sojourns into nonacademic settings such as planning and housing agencies and medical research. He has conducted research on urban problems, the social stratification system, mass communications, and popular culture. Gans currently works at the Center for Policy Research in New York City.

Perhaps Gans's most influential work has been his research in the area of community. His two most famous studies are of an established community, *The Urban Villagers,* and of an emerging community, *The Levittowners.* The first describes a declining section of South Boston that contained a number of Italian ethnic families who maintained their own integrated culture in the face of neighborhood disorganization. The ethnographic description contained in *The Urban Villagers* runs counter to the model of urban neighborhood disorganization found in the writings of the Chicago school. Gans noted the importance of primary relationships for the day-to-day functioning of the urban villagers. Regardless of their ethnicity, families of working- and middle-class backgrounds seemed to share many commonalities, an observation that complemented his idea of social class as an important variable in family structure.

Gans's description of the new residents of Levittown also runs counter to the legacy in the sociological literature. Unlike other observers, he remarks that suburbanites are not necessarily conformist in nature, that rather than forming one mass group, they differentiate themselves into informal groupings such as social class, age, or religion. The description reminds us that the human element is still paramount in determining a sense of community—a lesson that should be well noted by planners of new towns and housing developments.

An interesting thread running through Gans's work is the meaning of place of residence. He probes what a move to the suburbs means to individuals recently transplanted from cities and urban areas, and he analyzes what city residence means to different types of urban dwellers.

Gans's work is respected for its methodology as well as its content. He is a master of the participant observation tradition.

ERVING GOFFMAN

A strong advocate of the symbolic interactionist perspective as developed by Herbert Blumer, Erving Goffman received his Ph.D. in sociology from the University of Chicago. He has taught at the University of California at Berkeley and at the University of Pennsylvania. In 1961 he received the Robert MacIver award from the American Sociological Association.

A consistent theme in Goffman's published work is the emergence of individual self-concepts through everyday social interaction and experience. He uses the term "impression management" to describe how individuals or actors present themselves and the image they wish to project to various others in society. Much social interaction, he notes, deals with individuals and their attempts to impress and influence others.

In addition to his discussions on the emergence of self, Goffman has shared his thoughts on socialization and complex organizations, as he does in *Asylums: Essays on the Social Situation of Mental Patients and Other Inmates.* His concept of the "total institution" has stimulated research on organizations such as mental hospitals, prisons, and the military. He used the term to refer to institutions that seek exclusive control over the lives of their members. To gain it, they avoid the traditional separation of work, leisure, and sleep, blending their members' activities together in a process that is designed to change the members in some way. These institutions, according to Goffman, are characterized by: an internal division between staff and inmates; the need for incentives to induce members to cooperate in goal attainment activities; and the unusual character of their main work, generally aimed at changing the members in some way.

In *Asylums,* Goffman calls attention to the socialization process used in total institutions. He refers to the process as "mortification," a term that describes the way in which these institutions systematically destroy the inmates' existing concepts of self. It refers to the methods used by prisons, the military, and other institutions to blend individuals into a single type of person, totally dependent on the organization for an identity. Goffman's descriptive accounts reveal the informal operations of coercive organizations. Students of numerous subfields within sociology will find his work stimulating.

ALVIN W. GOULDNER

A native of New York City, Alvin W. Gouldner received his Ph.D. in sociology from Columbia University in 1953. He is the founder of *Trans Action Magazine* and a former president of the Society for the Study of Social Problems. He served as a Distinguished Professor of Sociological Theory at Washington University in St. Louis.

Gouldner is known primarily for his work in applied social science and organizational analysis. Among his published volumes are *Studies in Leadership; Patterns of Industrial Bureaucracy; Wildcat Strike;* and *The Coming Crisis in Western Sociology.*

One of Gouldner's contributions to the treasure chest of sociological concepts is his distinction between cosmopolitans and locals, a distinction he originally developed in reference to college faculty. Although this ideal model has been seriously questioned by recent scholars, it has served as a basis for much empirical investigation into professionalism and role orientation. Cosmopolitans are attuned to the issues of their wider profession, and they use a wider network of professional contacts than those available at their local institution. Locals on the other hand are more attentive to issues confronting their home institution.

Gouldner's writing on bureaucracy alerts us to some pressing issues in organizational analysis. He reminds us of the necessity for understanding the social environment in which organizations exist, for the value system of the individual, shaped by extra-organizational concerns, may conflict with the rational emphasis of the bureaucracy. He cautions that if organizations hope to survive, they must become aware of and utilize existing informal and traditional practices. In *Patterns of Industrial Bureaucracy,* Gouldner discusses how relations between workers, management, and the outside community of a gypsum plant are affected by various aspects of bureaucratization. He outlines differences between mock, representative, and punishment-centered bureaucracy.

Gouldner's desire to close the gap between pure and applied sociology is evidenced in *Wildcat Strike,* where he again assumes a functionalist perspective to describe a strike, to explain the circumstances leading to it, and to develop a framework for the study of group tension.

Sociology as a discipline has also been of interest to Gouldner. He contrasts various traditions in sociology, such as the conflict between the value-free proponents and the more radical advocates of value espousal. He warns sociologists against becoming entrapped by various funding agencies and attendant special interests.

GEORGE C. HOMANS

George C. Homans, a professor of sociology at Harvard since 1953, is a functionalist theorist who has developed a conceptual scheme very much in the tradition of his Harvard colleague Talcott Parsons. He served as president of the American Sociological Association from 1963 to 1964. In fact, Professor Homans is unique in that he is the only sociologist without a Ph.D. ever to hold that office.

Although he is viewed as a theoretician, much of Homans's work has had practical significance. The ideas in *The Human Group* and in *Social Behavior: Its Elementary Forms* have been applied repeatedly by students of group structure and function and by persons working in related fields such as industrial relations or social work.

The Human Group, a classic in the field, consists of a series of studies based on Homans's observation of groups. From these studies he abstracted commonalities which he presented in propositional form. In *Social Behavior,* Homans reports on several experimental studies of groups and group activities. He drew heavily upon the theory of exchange relationships to explore individual motivations in interaction. By considering nonrational elements in human interaction, Homans has made sociologists more aware of the informal elements of social life.

Group leadership is one of Homans's most productive areas of inquiry. He studied the functions of leaders rather than their personality attributes, and he discovered that leaders generally embody the group's normative system. A leader controls the group and is in turn controlled by it. In the latter case we are reminded that the leader must conform to the group's normative expectations if he is to maintain his position. Homans noted how leadership and social status relate in terms of society's willingness to reward its leaders.

The system that Homans utilized to explore human group behavior rested on the mutual dependence of the variables of sentiment, activity, and interaction. The system allows us to understand

GEORGE C. HOMANS

many factors associated with the formation of group identities and boundaries in society. For example, the model postulates that favorable sentiments as expressed in the pursuit of common activities promote differentiation of groups in society. The proposition that intensive interaction increases sentiment seems to have much relevance for improving the quality of social life.

MIRRA KOMAROVSKY

Born in Russia, Mirra Komarovsky received her Ph.D. in sociology from Columbia University. She has worked at the Social Sciences Research Council at Columbia and has taught at Barnard College, from which she received her undergraduate degree. She served as president of the American Sociological Association from 1972 to 1973.

Komarovsky's research interests have centered on the sociology of the family, sex roles, and social stratification. Her initial research, however, was on the use of leisure time, an area that she explored during her career as a doctoral student at Columbia. Her interests mirror those of one of her teachers at Columbia, Robert Lynd.

Komarovsky has examined sex role conflicts of both males and females. *The Unemployed Man and His Family* discusses the conflicts experienced by males when they are forced to assume a dependent role or one that does not fulfill the dominant cultural expectation. *Women in the Modern World* also looks at breaches of the cultural expectation of sex roles, this time from the perspective of emerging modern womanhood.

In 1964 Komarovsky completed an account of the family life and personality development of working-class people. Entitled *Blue Collar Marriage,* the volume explores social class value systems and perspectives. The term "marriage of convenience" aptly describes marital arrangements of participants in Komarovsky's survey; that is, as long as the families remained intact and enjoyed some semblance of financial security, the working or blue-collar respondents were relatively satisfied. Komarovsky's findings approximated those of William Whyte in *Street Corner Society* and Herbert Gans in *The Urban Villagers* in that she too saw blue-collar husbands and wives leading relatively separate

MIRRA KOMAROVSKY

lives in which each partner spends large blocks of leisure time with friends of the same sex. Komarovsky points out that values associated with stereotypes of marital happiness do not apply to the blue-collar perception of marriage.

PAUL F. LAZARSFELD

Paul F. Lazarsfeld, who died during the 1976 annual meeting of the American Sociological Association, was one of the founders of modern sociology. Besides being an intellectual force in the field, he was also the foremost proponent of applied research centers and institutes.

Lazarsfeld was born in 1901 in Vienna, Austria, where he also began his academic life. In 1925 he received a Ph.D. in mathematics, but immediately thereafter he was attracted to social psychology and the work of the Buhlers in Vienna. Lazarsfeld came to the United States following brief employment as an interpreter in France. His early academic career in the United States included short sojourns at the University of Newark and at Princeton University. In both instances there were early evidences and prototypes of his now famous Bureau of Applied Social Research at Columbia University.

Most of Lazarsfeld's early empirical research was in the area of mass communications. *Radio Research* and *Personal Influence* marked him as an important contributor to audience and market research theory and methodology. The latter work is also useful to students of social change and innovation. Sophisticated sharpening of survey research methodology for causal inference is a direct result of Lazarsfeld's work. His election studies, *The People's Choice* and *Voting,* legitimated the subfield of political sociology by introducing such techniques as panel analysis and by giving new methodological direction to survey research.

Mathematical sociology is another area that owes a debt to Paul Lazarsfeld. His *Latent Structure Analysis* is considered a classic, and his mathematical sociology lectures at the Bureau of Applied Social Research shaped the development of this field throughout the 1960s.

Lazarsfeld's interests were not limited to the aforementioned areas. *Academic Mind,* for example, is a classic study of higher education and differences and motivations within that sacrosanct segment of American society. Again, the work is noted for both substantive content and methodological innovation. Because of his keen interest in the organization of research in higher education, Lazarsfeld also helped establish university research centers worldwide. At the time of his death he was again at the edge of a new frontier in sociology. He headed the new and exciting applied sociology program at the University of Pittsburgh.

The influence of Paul Lazarsfeld on modern sociology was acknowledged in his lifetime, for he was honored by numerous sociological organizations, including the American Sociological Association, which made him its president. His influence is most apparent, though, in the works of his students, some of whom, like C. Wright Mills, also attained highest recognition in the field.

SEYMOUR M. LIPSET

Seymour M. Lipset, born in New York in 1922, is one of the most prolific scholars in modern sociology. He received his Ph.D. from Columbia University in 1949 and has subsequently taught sociology and political science courses at the University of Toronto, the University of California at Berkeley, and at Columbia, Harvard, and Stanford Universities. Lipset received the MacIver Award of the American Sociological Association in 1962. Although his research covers a multiplicity of topics, his main areas of interest have been comparative politics, the politics of intellectuals, social stratification, and higher education.

The book *Political Man* demonstrates how integrated Lipset's varied research interests are. In this volume he linked the social stratification system to the system of political control. In his preference for an order model of society, he documented how individuals in society seek rewards, but he acknowledged that for the system's sake there must be an institutionalized inequality. Echoing Robert Michels's iron law of oligarchy, Lipset argued that in a stratified society with differential power between the strata, members of the more powerful strata seek to enhance and maintain their position. He recognized the pressures resulting from stratified inequality and assigned political institutions the task of dealing with these pressures. Here and elsewhere in his work,

Lipset discusses voting behavior. Analysis of voting is valuable, he says, because voting is both a mechanism of consensus in democratic societies and a way of institutionalizing group conflict.

In examining the relationship between voting behavior and social stratification, Lipset actually worked from a central concern of Marxist social analysis. He isolated the factors that lead to individual and group support of political movements or parties objectively linked to their class interests. In *Social Mobility in Industrial Society,* Lipset and Reinhard Bendix undertook a cross-cultural study of this type of relationship. They found much variation: American and British workers have a lower electoral participation rate than middle-class individuals, but their counterparts in certain German and Austrian cities have a higher participation rate. The authors attributed the discrepancy to differences in socialization as well as to the presence of institutionalized class networks in the German and Austrian cities. They concluded that electoral participation by workers is due not to socioeconomic variables alone, but also to the presence of integrated class networks coupled with status.

Lipset himself has completed several studies on the occupation and political behavior of trade union members, sociologists, and the American academic community. An early work, *Union Democracy,* deserves mention for both its substantive and methodological content. The framework of Robert Michels's iron law of oligarchy is evident again in this study of the International Typographical Union. Lipset traced the structural factors that led to a seemingly democratic union in which statuses of leaders and rank and file were not as disparate as those typically found between such groups. He also examined characteristics associated with union activism. The analysis proceeds on both an individual and a group level. The appendix of the book details the methodological challenges of the work; it contains valuable insights for beginning students and seasoned researchers.

Democracy as a social phenomenon is a major theme in much of Lipset's work. He examined economic development and political legitimacy as cross-societal requisites for democracy, and he applied the Parsonian pattern-variables to an analysis of the values of several democratic societies.

SEYMOUR M. LIPSET

A very important book by Lipset is *The First New Nation.*
Here again he applied the Parsonian pattern-variables, this time
to an analysis of underlying societal values. He examined society
in terms of the concept of legitimacy and the Weberian explication thereof. Lipset discussed what he considers to be enduring
values culled from a historical analysis of the American social
structure.

Lipset's concern with social structure and social inequality
prompted him to study many American and cross-societal institutions. He has expanded upon some earlier theoretical formula-
tions in sociology, notably those from Weber. His comparative
work and his numerous individual case studies combine to make
sociology a richer discipline.

ROBERT MERTON

Robert Merton must be regarded as a giant in twentieth-century
sociology. Merton was born in Philadelphia, Pennsylvania, in
1910. He taught at Harvard, where he also earned his doctorate
in sociology, and at Tulane before joining the faculty of Columbia
University where, along with Paul Lazarsfeld, he headed the Bureau of Applied Social Research.

Merton's interests in sociology span a number of areas of inquiry. His research concentrates on the sociology of science, with
focus on the interaction of cognitive and social structures in various disciplines, and on structural analysis in sociology, with focus
on role-sets and status-sets. He is best known for his contributions to sociological theory and in particular for his development
of middle-range theories. Merton has made sociological theory
meaningful in everyday life by using it to analyze social problems.

One example of Merton's application of theory can be seen in
his approach to the theory of anomie. He attempted to show how
deviant behavior may be the expected result of the pressures of
the social structure operating on given social groups. He contended that the same forces that produce conformity also produce
deviation. These forces are generally construed as pressures to
achieve cultural goals.

His theory of anomie contains five possible adaptations to cultural means and cultural goals. The first, conformity, exists when

ROBERT MERTON

175

an individual has accepted both the cultural goals and the pre-
scribed means to reach them; such a person is not likely to de-
viate. When the cultural goals are accepted but the means to
reach them are not, the adaptation is labeled innovation. An example of this type of deviance might be embezzlement as performed in the course of a white-collar occupation. When a person
fails to meet his goals but continues to abide slavishly by the pre-
scribed rules, ritualism occurs. As an example, Merton holds up
the behavior of the low-level or first-line bureaucrat who, strangled
by red tape, happily wraps the same about the neck of his clients.
In this schema a suicide victim, who rejects both the goals and
the means to reach them, is labeled a retreatist. The fifth adaptation is rebellion. Rebellion occurs when a person rejects cultural means and goals and replaces them with new ones. Counter-
movements such as revolts are typical of this type of response.
In the early 1960s a number of sociologists attempted to empirically verify Merton's typology and to apply it to an analysis of
various forms of deviant behavior.

Merton's book *Social Theory and Social Structure* deals with
a wide range of sociological topics and discusses the ideas of
several social theorists. In this work specific contributions are
made to the areas of social theory, social structure, the sociology
of knowledge, and the sociology of science. Merton provided terminology, such as latent and manifest function, which has served
as a basis for much of the structural functionalist approach to
society. By "latent function" he meant actual consequences, unin-
tended or unrecognized, of a social action or a series of actions,
which differ from the intended consequences. The intended or
ideal consequences he labeled "manifest function." Merton also
subscribed to the idea of a self-fulfilling prophecy based on W. I.
Thomas's concept of definition of the situation. Thomas had stated
that if men define situations as real, then they are real in their
consequences. For instance, if someone believes that another is
his worst enemy, the belief will cause the believer to behave in
hostile ways toward the other, and he in turn will behave in the
hypothesized fashion, thus fulfilling the prophecy.

The sociological term "role-set" is also attributed to Merton.
This term is used to indicate that a status may have more than

one role, i.e. a number of roles which fit together. A husband for example is also a son, sometimes a father, a neighbor, a tax payer. The multiplicity of roles in any one individual's set may place him in a conflict-laden situation. Merton was especially interested in this aspect of role conflict.

Students of decision making and social stratification have found Merton's differentiation between monomorphic and polymorphic spheres of influence to be useful. He steered sociological studies of the power variable away from monomorphic concerns and demonstrated that power could have many different forms.

Merton has made a wide-ranging contribution to the field of sociology. His impact is so vast that indeed it is difficult to gauge. Subfields like complex organizations are richer for his descriptive data such as that on the bureaucratic personality and the function of rules in large organizations. The sociology of science owes him a debt for hypothesizing causal relationships in the discovery, invention, and diffusion of knowledge and ideas. Students have found his middle-range theorizing a more realistic and meaningful attempt than many of the broader overarching system theories. He represents a unique American adaptation to sociology: limited theorizing based on careful empirical and historical research. His influence, especially on a whole generation of Columbia sociology graduates, will have a vast impact on the future of American sociology.

ROBERT A. NISBET

The occupant of the distinguished Albert Schweitzer Chair in the Humanities at Columbia University, Robert Nisbit is an expert sociologist on the general topics of social organization and social change and development. He received his Ph.D. from the University of California at Berkeley in 1939 and has authored several important volumes in sociology.

Nisbet's first major volume has become a classic in the area of community study. Initially titled *Quest for Community,* the work was later retitled *Community and Power.* In contrasting traditional *Gemeinschaft* forms of social organization as found in feudal castes and medieval society with modern, *Gesellschaft* forms, Nisbet relies heavily on the framework of Ferdinand Toennies. He comments on the rootlessness and apparent social anomie of individuals in societies characterized by increased rationality and formal social relationships. He also laments the fact that people in modern society are less likely to relate with their neighbors or identify with their communities. Some sociologists feel that he is being overly nostalgic about former social conditions without having a true appreciation of new forms of community and social organization. Nisbet maintains that the future of democracy depends on the ability of society to construct networks of loyalties and associations that will act as checks on a growing tendency toward centralized commitment and authority. He asserts the need for a more genuine sense of community to overcome the insecurity that he attributes to a weakening of community life in modern society.

The Social Bond, written in 1970, is an important work on social change. Nisbet stresses that social structures cannot control or determine the totality of human social behavior that occurs within them. He picks events as the major factor in social change, but he points out that their random nature has made sociologists and others reluctant to explain social change in terms of events. This volume also deals with cooperation (for which Nisbet developed a fourfold typology), conflict, and other social processes.

Nisbet's book *Sociology as an Art Form* is a most intriguing essay which criticizes existing theory and methodology in sociology and draws an analogy between sociology and art rather than science. Nisbet sees the forms of sociology as identical to those of art. Just as an artist paints a landscape of the countryside, the sociologist constructs landscapes of his subject matter. The book is sure to provoke criticism from those sociologists who are certain that their purpose is to capture reality and not to fantasize in a way permitted the artist. The thesis is, however, interesting and certain to be fuel for those who seek to keep the discipline responsive to its critics.

Nisbet's thesis may also serve to revive some interest in retaining the vestigial remains of the social philosophy component of the discipline. In brief, mainstream sociology involves a relatively strict empirical approach to reality which limits the field of inquiry by automatically ruling out certain types of questions. Obviously not all questions of a social nature, no matter how important, can be addressed in a truly scientific fashion. Sociologists have long sought full acceptance of the discipline as a science. In working to achieve that end, some potential inquiries have been ignored simply because of inadequate methodology. As a result, the field of inquiry may have been unduly trivialized.

Nisbet suggests that there is a need for imagination and creativity in sociology, and, it might be added, in science itself. Whether or not one agrees with his point of view, his work merits serious consideration.

TALCOTT PARSONS

The most comprehensive attempt by an American sociologist at developing a general theory of society is that undertaken by Talcott Parsons. Born in 1902, he graduated from Amherst College and studied at the London School of Economics and Heidelberg University. He completed his doctorate on capitalism at Heidelberg and returned to Amherst, where he taught economics. He taught economics and sociology at Harvard as well.

The economist Pareto and the sociologist Weber both influenced the direction of Parsons's early work, which tried to synthesize economics and sociology. In 1946 the Department of Social Relations was created at Harvard, and Parsons became its first chairman. Reflected in his work are the ideas of sociologists such as Weber and Durkheim, of Sigmund Freud, the father of psychoanalysis, and, most of all, of the economist Alfred Marshall. Marshall, like Parsons, was interested in a more general theory of social systems.

In 1937 Parsons published *The Structure of Social Action,* a review of major existing social theories and an initial attempt to build a framework for a general theory of social action. His theory of action rejected earlier conceptions of self-interest as the dominant source of order in social life. It rested instead on an examination of the normative aspects of social life. He viewed action as rooted in norms and bounded by value principles.

In his writing, Parsons has always advocated a broad-based system theory. He has opposed the trend of social interpretation that is based simply on empirical generalization and has urged theorists and researchers to look beyond their observations, to probe the possible relationship between a wide array of social phenomena. Spearheading the search for universals in social life, he encouraged the scientist to join him in constructing an integrated, systematic scheme to relate these variables. Parsons is most often criticized for vagaries or problems that appear in his work when he brings his theoretical statements to bear on an empirical level.

In his search for system universals Parsons delineated three analytic systems to be used in the analysis of existing societies. These are the personality, social, and cultural systems. The first system refers to characteristics peculiar to an individual that affect his functioning in social life; the second refers to patterns and units of interaction; and the cultural system encompasses cognitive, evaluative, and symbolic aspects of the action system. Action is the basis of understanding the relationship between personality and the social system. Underlying the personality system are individual needs, which limit the range of possibilities of human behavior. Parsons placed the individual organism at the bottom of a hierarchy of systems. Personality, the control agent of the organism, is the next highest level. These are controlled in turn by the social and cultural systems in a hierarchical arrangement.

Parsons contends that individuals in the social system always act as individuals in a role. Individual action, he said, can be analyzed in terms of roles or systems of solidarity that give meaning to the role. These in turn are constrained by aspects of the social and cultural situation. It has been Parsons's aim to delineate all the structures and processes that impinge upon action. Since individuals always act in terms of a role, he views interaction as being organized about a system of roles which are further organized into systems of collectivities. Roles and collectivities as basic units of the social system are defined by norms and values. Norms are legal prescriptions or less formal agreements of procedure, while values act as general principles or

TALCOTT PARSONS

181

guides for behavior. Parsons conceives roles, collectivities, norms, and values as basic components of a social system. They are in a hierarchical relationship, with values being in the highest order. Some criticism has been leveled at Parsons in this regard, since the exact nature of the relationship between norms and values can be questioned. It is unclear whether or not norms support and implement socially shared system values. In Parsons's scheme it becomes necessary for values to become patterned or regularized in society as well as internalized by individual personalities.

Three aspects of action were discussed by Parsons: the cognitive, cathectic, and value orientation. The last-named gives rise to his famous "pattern variables," standards for social action. These variables, universalism versus particularism, achievement versus ascription, affectivity versus affective neutrality, and specificity versus diffuseness, have been used to analyze social interaction in a variety of settings. In *The Social System* Parsons developed a full explanation of the pattern variables. Students of modernization and development, complex organizations, the family, and occupations and professions have found these variables useful for analytic and descriptive purposes.

System structure became the focus of Parsons's work as he began to elaborate on a functional subsystem model designed to elucidate the problems faced by all social systems, namely, problems of commitment to values, system integration, goal achievement, and adaptation to environment.

Despite his preference for system theorizing, Parsons has applied his insights to a number of social issues. His writings on the sick role and the social aspects of health and sickness are indispensable to students interested in medical sociology or the sociology of health. His theoretical conceptions have been applied to such topics as deviance, education, and the role of religion. He has influenced many leading sociologists, including Smelser, Bellah, Lipset, Einsenstadt, and Etzioni. His more recent work on modernization is proving invaluable in the study of third-world development.

Parsons has been criticized for his jargon and for his seeming inability to make theoretical and empirical linkages. A humorous scene occurred at a meeting of the American Sociological Association in the late 1960s, when Parsons was asked by a colleague to hold a large cardboard sketch of a 2 x 2 contingency table. Several individuals in the audience chuckled at this sight, remarking that this would be the one and only time in his life that Parsons permitted himself to be seen with the trappings of an empirical methodologist. However, one cannot detract from the contribution that Parsons has made. He has helped move the social sciences, especially economics and sociology, closer together. Above all, he has fostered the comparative examination of social systems and the various subsystems within them. He has provided sociology with an identity and strengthened its claim as a science. Talcott Parsons died in May 1979.

DAVID RIESMAN

Riesman's sociology represents a unique inquiry into the character of American institutions and culture. He was originally trained as a lawyer, having served a clerkship under Justice Brandeis. He was also a deputy assistant district attorney of New York County and a professor of law at the University of Chicago and at Harvard.

Riesman's early works—*The Lonely Crowd* and *Faces in the Crowd*—centered upon man's early search for identity against the forces of alienation in modern society. He discussed sources of direction in man's search for identity. The first source of guidance is tradition, which is usually looked to in a period of slow growth and change. It illustrates how things should be done, because what worked in the past is assumed to work also in the present. Riesman labeled as tradition-directed those people who during earlier eras used ancestors as a reference in coping with present problems. However, when change in society is accelerated, these earlier solutions may not work well. Parents and other socialization agents try to give children a set of principles to help them work out solutions to life's problems. These internal principles, Riesman said, result in a sense of inner-direction. When the tradition-directed man feels that he has fallen short of the expectations of his traditional community, he will, Riesman hypothesized, feel a sense of shame. The inner-directed man, on the other hand,

DAVID RIESMAN

184

will experience guilt because he has not fulfilled the goals held out to him in early socialization. As social change increases, these mechanisms must be replaced with new, other-directed responses.

The distinctive feature of other-directed societies is that the source of direction is one's contemporaries. The contemporaries need not be known personally, for their way of life and values can be perceived through media and other sources. In complex societies individuals see that there are various ways of coping with problems and that other people become just as committed to a way of life as they are. Not knowing how one is to act in a rapidly changing situation, or which rule to employ therein, results not in shame or guilt, but in anxiety. It seems that in the other-directed society there is no one correct response in individuals' adaptations. Rather, as Riesman's title implies, the individual is alone; he is lonely, even in a crowd. Riesman's typology has facilitated the empirical study of social change. Since it was intended to be an ideal typical description rather than an encompassing description of social change, one cannot criticize it too severely. He has captured some aspects of social change as societies develop in more complex directions. It remains for the social psychologist to evaluate the aspects of his work that deal with psychological mechanisms dominant in the various periods. Researchers seeking empirical evidence for theories of loneliness and alienation have used Riesman's discussion as a starting point.

In his analysis of the character of American institutions Riesman has turned his attention to education, and to higher education in particular. Ideologically, he advocates a return to a more conservative form of education that would include certain standard core subjects. He displays a tremendous insight into the differences among American colleges and universities. One of his more important pieces of writing on this topic is *Constraint and Variety in American Education*. His essay "The Academic Procession" discusses the relations between the elite of American colleges, the middle group, and the bottom rung of the hierarchy. He argues that education is at its best when it guards against dominant trends and fashions of the time, whether progressive or conservative.

ROBIN M. WILLIAMS

To understand the structure of American society has been a lifelong pursuit of sociologist Robin M. Williams. Born in North Carolina in 1914, Williams did graduate work in sociology at the University of North Carolina, Cornell, and Harvard University. He received his Ph.D. from Harvard in 1943 and has been a member of the sociology faculty at Cornell for more than thirty years. In addition to his skill as a sociologist, Williams is an exemplary humanitarian and teacher.

Williams's research has concentrated on social organization, intergroup relations and conflict, and values. His major effort is embodied in the book *American Society: A Sociological Interpretation*. Its strength derives from the way in which Williams integrates seemingly diverse pieces of information to arrive at a synthesis of the values and principles underlying the American social system. Unlike many other writers, Williams does not seek merely to describe American society, but to understand it as well. He explains how the structure and function of several major institutions in the United States interrelate to form a system.

Sociologists rely heavily on Williams's description of the American value system. He perceives American culture as characterized by the following characteristics: it is organized around active mastery; it is manipulative of the external world as opposed to being centered on inner experience; it emphasizes rationality as opposed to tradition; it has a dimension of orderliness; it follows a universal as opposed to particular ethic; it emphasizes equality as opposed to hierarchy; and it is concerned with individual personality rather than group bonds. His list of characteristically American values gives highest priority to freedom and includes: personal achievement, work, moralism, efficiency, progress, equality, and patriotism. *American Society* is necessary reading for any student who hopes to understand the continuity of American social institutions.

Other research by Williams is also of sociological relevance. His early research with Edward Suchman, Paul Lazarsfeld, and others on the social psychology of the American soldier during World

ROBIN M. WILLIAMS

187

War II, as well as his recent work on factors involved in inter-group conflict, should not be dismissed. A somewhat overlooked study is his *Strangers Next Door,* a study of prejudice and authoritarianism in modern society. Williams devotes special attention to power differentials in society and the importance of class and mobility in assessing life chances.

Selected
Bibliography

Allport, Gordon W. *The Nature of Prejudice.* Garden City, N.Y.: Doubleday, 1958.

Allport, Gordon W., and Barry M. Kramer. "Some Roots of Prejudice." *Journal of Psychology* 22 (1946): 9–39.

Allport, Gordon W., and Allen Postman. *The Psychology of Rumor.* New York: Henry Holt, 1947.

Becker, Howard S. *The Outsiders.* New York: Free Press, 1963.

Becker, Howard S. *The Other Side.* New York: Free Press, 1964.

Becker, Howard S., and Blanche Geer. "The Fate of Idealism in Medical Schools." *American Sociological Review* 23 (1958): 50–56.

Bell, Daniel. "The Power Elite Reconsidered." *American Journal of Sociology* 64 (1958): 238–250.

Bell, Daniel. *The End of Ideology.* New York: Free Press, 1960.

Bell, Daniel. *The Coming of Post-Industrial Society.* New York: Basic Books, 1973.

Bell, Daniel. *The Cultural Contradictions of Capitalism.* New York: Basic Books, 1976.

Bendix, Reinhard. *Work and Authority in Industry.* New York: John Wiley, 1956.

Bendix, Reinhard. *Max Weber: An Intellectual Portrait.* Garden City, N.Y.: Doubleday, 1960.

Bendix, Reinhard, and S. M. Lipset. "Political Sociology." *Current Sociology* 6 (1957): 79–99.

Bendix, Reinhard, and S. M. Lipset, eds. *Class, Status and Power.* New York: Free Press, 1953.

Benedict, Ruth. *The Concept of the Guardian Spirit in North America.* American Anthropological Association, Memoir no. 29, 1923.

Benedict, Ruth. "Configurations of Culture in North America." *American Anthropologist* 34 (1932): 1–27.

Benedict, Ruth. "Continuities and Discontinuities in Cultural Conditioning." *Psychiatry* 1 (1938): 161–167.

Benedict, Ruth. *The Chrysanthemum and the Sword: Patterns of Japanese Culture.* Boston: Houghton Mifflin, 1946.

Benedict, Ruth. *Patterns of Culture.* Boston: Houghton Mifflin, 1959.

189

Berger, Peter L. *Invitation to Sociology*. Garden City, N.Y.: Doubleday, Anchor, 1963.

Berger, Peter L. *Pyramids of Sacrifice: Political Ethics and Social Change*. New York: Basic Books, 1975.

Berger, Peter L., and Thomas Luckmann. *The Social Construction of Reality*. London: Penguin Press, 1967.

Berger, Peter L., and Brigitte Berger. *Sociology, a Biographical Approach*. rev. ed. New York: Basic Books, 1975.

Blau, Peter, and Richard Scott. *Formal Organizations*. San Francisco: Chandler Publishing Co., 1962.

Blau, Peter. *Exchange and Power in Social Life*. New York: John Wiley, 1964.

Blau, Peter. "The Study of Formal Organization." In *American Sociology*, edited by Talcott Parsons. New York: Basic Books, 1968.

Blau, Peter. *The Dynamics of Bureaucracy*. Rev. ed. Chicago: University of Chicago Press, 1973.

Burgess, Ernest; Harvey J. Locke; and Mary Margaret Thomes. *The Family: From Institution to Companionship*. 2nd ed. New York: American Book Co., 1953.

Burgess, Ernest, ed. *Aging in Western Societies*. Chicago: University of Chicago Press, 1960.

Chapin, F. Stuart. *Experimental Designs in Social Research*. New York: Harper & Row, 1947.

Coleman, James S. *Community Conflict*. New York: Free Press, 1957.

Coleman, James S. *Adolescent Society*. New York: Free Press, 1961.

Coleman, James S. *Equality of Educational Opportunity*. Washington, D.C.: GPO, 1966.

Coleman, James S. "Community Disorganization and Conflict." In *Contemporary Social Problems*, edited by Robert K. Merton and Robert A. Nisbet. New York: Harcourt, Brace, Jovanovich, 1971.

Comte, Auguste. *The Positive Philosophy*. Translated by Harriet Martineau. New York: AMS Press, 1974.

Cooley, Charles H. "The Theory of Transportation." *Publications of the American Economic Association* 9 (1894).

Cooley, Charles H. *Human Nature and the Social Order*. New York: Scribners Sons, 1902.

Cooley, Charles H. *Social Organization*. Edited by Elsie Jones Cooley. New York: Scribners Sons, 1937.

Coser, Lewis A. *The Functions of Social Conflict*. Glencoe, Ill.: Free Press, 1956.

Coser, Lewis A. "Functions of Deviant Behavior." *American Journal of Sociology* 68 (1962): 172–182.

Coser, Lewis A. *Masters of Sociological Thought*. New York: Harcourt, Brace, Jovanovich, 1971.

Cressey, Donald R. *The Prison: Studies in Institutional Organization and Change.* New York: Holt, Rinehart & Winston, 1961.

Cressey, Donald R., and David A. Ward. *Delinquency, Crime and Social Process.* New York: Harper & Row, 1969.

Cressey, Donald R. *Theft of the Nation.* New York: Harper & Row, 1969.

Cressey, Donald R. *Other People's Money.* Belmont, Calif.: Wadsworth, 1971.

Cressey, Donald R. *Criminal Organization: Its Elementary Forms.* New York: Harper & Row, 1972.

Dahrendorf, Ralf. "Toward a Theory of Social Conflict." *Journal of Conflict Resolution* 11 (1958): 170–183.

Dahrendorf, Ralf. *Class and Class Conflict in Industrial Society.* Stanford, Calif.: Stanford University Press, 1959.

Dahrendorf, Ralf. "Out of Utopia: Toward a Reorientation of Sociological Analysis." In *Change and Conflict,* edited by N. J. Demerath and Richard Peterson. New York: Free Press, 1967.

Darwin, Charles. *The Descent of Man and Selection in Relation to Sex.* New York: D. Appleton, 1872.

Darwin, Charles. *The Origin of the Species.* New York: P. F. Collier, 1909.

Davis, Kingsley. *Human Society.* New York: Macmillan, 1949.

Davis, Kingsley. "Prostitution" and "The World's Population Crisis." Both in *Contemporary Social Problems,* 2nd ed. Edited by Robert Merton and Robert Nisbet. New York: Harcourt, Brace and World, 1966.

Davis, Kingsley, and Wilbert E. Moore. "Some Principles of Stratification." *American Sociological Review* 10 (1945): 242–249.

Dewey, John. *Democracy and Education.* New York: Macmillan, 1916.

Dewey, John. *Experience and Education.* New York: Macmillan, 1938.

Durkheim, Emile. *The Elementary Forms of Religious Life.* London: G. Allen, 1912.

Durkheim, Emile. *Rules of the Sociological Method.* Translated by Sarah A. Solovay and John H. Mueller. Edited by George E. G. Catlin. New York: Free Press, 1938.

Durkheim, Emile. *Suicide: A Study in Sociology.* Translated by John A. Spaulding and George Simpson. New York: Free Press, 1951.

Durkheim, Emile. *The Division of Labor in Society.* New York: Free Press, 1960.

Etzioni, Amitai. *A Comparative Analysis of Complex Organizations.* New York: Free Press, 1961.

Etzioni, Amitai. *Modern Organization.* Englewood Cliffs, N.J.: Prentice-Hall, 1964.

Etzioni, Amitai. *The Active Society*. New York: Free Press, 1968.

Etzioni, Amitai. *A Sociological Reader on Complex Organizations*. New York: Holt, Rinehart & Winston, 1970.

Etzioni, Amitai. *Genetic Fix*. New York: Macmillan, 1973.

Freud, Sigmund. *A General Introduction to Psychoanalysis*. New York: Horace Liveright, 1920.

Freud, Sigmund. *Totem and Taboo*. Translated by A. A. Brill. New York: Random House, 1946.

Freud, Sigmund. *Civilization and Its Discontents*. Translated by James Stracney. New York: Norton, 1961.

Fromm, Erich. *Escape from Freedom*. New York: Holt, Rinehart & Winston, 1941.

Fromm, Erich. *Man for Himself*. New York: Holt, Rinehart & Winston, 1947.

Fromm, Erich. *The Art of Loving*. New York: Harper, 1956.

Gans, Herbert H. "Urbanism and Suburbanism as Ways of Life: A Reevaluation of Definitions." In *Human Behavior and Social Processes,* edited by Arnold Ross. Boston: Houghton Mifflin, 1962.

Gans, Herbert H. *The Urban Villagers*. New York: Free Press, 1965.

Gans, Herbert H. *The Levittowners: How People Live and Politic in Suburbia*. New York: Pantheon, 1966.

Gans, Herbert H. *Popular Culture and High Culture: An Analysis and Evaluation of Taste*. New York: Basic Books, 1974.

Gerth, Hans H., and C. Wright Mills, eds. and trans. *From Max Weber: Essays in Sociology*. New York: Oxford University Press, 1946.

Giddings, Franklin H. *The Principles of Sociology*. New York: Macmillan, 1896.

Giddings, Franklin H. *Democracy and Empire*. New York: Macmillan, 1900.

Giddings, Franklin H. *Industrial Sociology*. New York: Macmillan, 1901.

Giddings, Franklin H. *Readings in Descriptive and Historical Sociology*. New York: Macmillan, 1923.

Goffman, Erving. *The Presentation of Self in Everyday Society*. Garden City, N.Y.: Doubleday, 1959.

Goffman, Erving. *Asylums: Essays on the Social Situation of Mental Patients and Other Inmates*. Garden City, N.Y.: Doubleday, 1961.

Goode, William J. "The Sociology of the Family." In *Sociology Today,* edited by Robert K. Merton. New York: Basic Books, 1958.

Goode, William J. *World Revolution and Family Patterns*. New York: Free Press, 1963.

Goode, William J. *The Family*. Englewood Cliffs, N.J.: Prentice-Hall, 1964.

Goode, William J., and Paul K. Hatt. *Methods in Social Research.* New York: McGraw-Hill, 1952.

Gouldner, Alvin W. "Metaphysical Pathos and the Theory of Bureaucracy." *The American Political Science Review* 49 (1955): 496–507.

Gouldner, Alvin W. *Patterns of Industrial Bureaucracy.* New York: Free Press, 1954.

Gouldner, Alvin W. "Cosmopolitans and Locals: Towards an Analysis of Latent Social Roles." *Administrative Science Quarterly* 2 (1957): 281–92.

Gouldner, Alvin W. *Wildcat Strike.* New York: Harper Torchbooks, 1965.

Gouldner, Alvin W. *The Coming Crisis in Western Sociology.* New York: Basic Books, 1970.

Gouldner, Alvin W., and S. M. Miller, eds. *Applied Sociology: Opportunities and Problems.* New York: Free Press, 1965.

Hollingshead, August B. *Elmtown's Youth.* New York: John Wiley, 1949.

Hollingshead, August B. "Social Stratification and Psychiatric Disorders." *American Sociological Review* 18 (1953): 163-169.

Hollingshead, August B., and E. C. Redlich. *Social Class and Mental Illness.* New York: John Wiley, 1958.

Homans, George C. *The Human Group.* New York: Harcourt, Brace, Jovanovich, 1950.

Homans, George C. *The Nature of Social Science.* New York: Harcourt, Brace and World, 1967.

Homans, George C. *Social Behavior: Its Elementary Forms.* Rev. ed. New York: Harcourt, Brace, Jovanovich, 1974.

Hughes, Everett C. *French Canada in Transition.* Chicago: University of Chicago Press, 1943.

Hughes, Everett C. *Men and Their Work.* New York: Free Press, 1958.

Hughes, Everett C. *The Sociological Eye: Selected Papers on Work, Self and the Study of Society.* Chicago: Aldine, 1971.

Komarovsky, Mirra. *The Unemployed Man and His Family.* New York: Dryden, 1940.

Komarovsky, Mirra. "Cultural Contradictions and Sex Roles·" *American Journal of Sociology* 52 (1946): 184–189.

Komarovsky, Mirra. *Blue Collar Marriage.* New York: Random House, 1964.

Komarovsky, Mirra. "Cultural Contradictions and Sex Roles: The Masculine Case." *American Journal of Sociology* 78 (1973): 873–884.

Ladd, Everett Carl, and Seymour M. Lipset. *Professors, Unions and American Higher Education.* Washington: American Enterprise Institute for Public Policy Research, 1973.

Lazarsfeld, Paul F., and Wagner Thielens. *The People's Choice.* New York: Columbia University Press, 1948.

Lazarsfeld, Paul F., and Wagner Thielens. *The Academic Mind.* Glencoe, Ill.: Free Press, 1958.

Lazarsfeld, Paul F.; William H. Sewell; and Harold L. Wilensky, eds. *The Uses of Sociology.* New York: Basic Books, 1967.

Lazarsfeld, Paul F., and Morris Rosenberg, eds. *The Language of Social Research.* New York: Free Press, 1972.

Lazarsfeld, Paul F.; Ann Pasanella; and Morris Rosenberg, eds. *Continuities in the Language of Social Research.* New York: Free Press, 1972.

Lewin, Kurt. *Resolving Social Conflicts.* New York: Harper, 1948.

Lewin, Kurt. *The Field Theory in Social Science,* edited by D. Cartwright. New York: Harper, 1951.

Lewin, Kurt. "Group Decision and Social Change." In *Readings in Social Psychology,* edited by Macoby, Newcomb, and Hartley. New York: Holt, Rinehart & Winston, 1958.

Lipset, Seymour M. *Political Man.* Garden City, N.Y.: Doubleday, Anchor, 1963.

Lipset, Seymour M. *The First New Nation.* Garden City, N.Y.: Doubleday, Anchor, 1967.

Lipset, Seymour M.; Martin Trow; and James S. Coleman. *Union Democracy.* New York: Free Press, 1956.

Lipset, Seymour M., and Reinhart Bendix. *Social Mobility in Industrial Society.* Berkeley: University of California Press, 1960.

Lundberg, George A. *Can Science Save Us?* London: Longmans, Green, 1961.

Lynd, Robert S. *Knowledge for What?* Princeton: Princeton University Press, 1939.

Lynd, Robert S., and Helen M. Lynd. *Middletown.* New York: Harcourt, Brace & World, 1929.

Lynd, Robert S., and Helen M. Lynd. *Middletown in Transition.* New York: Harcourt, Brace & World, 1937.

Malinowski, Bronislaw. *Argonauts of the Western Pacific.* New York: E. P. Dutton, 1922.

Malinowski, Bronislaw. *Crime and Custom in Savage Society.* London: Routledge & Kegan Paul, 1926.

Malinowski, Bronislaw. *Sex and Repression in Savage Society.* New York: Harcourt, Brace & World, 1927.

Malinowski, Bronislaw. *Magic, Science and Religion.* New York: Free Press, 1948.

Malthus, Thomas. *Population: The First Essay.* Ann Arbor: University of Michigan Press, 1959.

Mannheim, Karl. *Man and Society in an Age of Reconstruction.* New York: Harcourt, Brace & World, 1940.

Mannheim, Karl. *Ideology and Utopia.* New York: Harcourt, Brace & Co., 1966.

Marx, Karl. *Das Kapital.* Edited by Friedrich Engels. Translated by Samuel Moore and Edward Aveling. London: G. Allen, 1946.

Marx, Karl, and Friedrich Engels. *Basic Writings on Politics and Philosophy.* Edited by Lewis S. Feuer. Garden City, N.Y.: Doubleday, 1959.

Mead, George H. *Mind, Self and Society.* Chicago: University of Chicago Press, 1934.

Mead, George H. "The Psychology of Punitive Justice." In *Sociological Theory: A Book of Readings,* edited by Lewis A. Coser and Bernard Rosenberg. New York: Macmillan, 1964.

Mead, Margaret. *Coming of Age in Samoa.* New York: William Morrow, 1928.

Mead, Margaret. *Male and Female.* New York: William Morrow 1949.

Mead, Margaret. *New Lives for Old: Cultural Transformation.* New York: William Morrow, 1956.

Mead, Margaret. *Cultural Patterns and Technical Change.* New York: UNESCO, Mentor Books, New American Library, 1956.

Mead, Margaret. *Culture and Commitment: A Study of the Generation Gap.* New York: Natural History Press, 1970.

Mead, Margaret. *Sex and Temperament in Three Primitive Societies.* New York: William Morrow, 1973.

Mead, Margaret, and Martha Wolfstein, eds. *Childhood in Contemporary Cultures.* Chicago: University of Chicago Press, 1955.

Merton, Robert. "Social Structure and Anomie." *American Sociology Review* 3 (1938): 672–82.

Merton, Robert. *Reader in Bureaucracy.* New York: Free Press, 1952.

Merton, Robert. *Social Theory and Social Structure.* New York: Free Press, 1968.

Merton, Robert. *Science, Technology and Society in 17th Century England.* New York: Free Press, 1970.

Merton, Robert, and Robert Nisbet, eds. *Contemporary Social Problems.* New York: Harcourt, Brace, Jovanovich, 1961.

Michels, Robert. *Political Parties.* New York: Free Press, 1949.

Mills, C. Wright, and Hans Gerth, eds. *From Max Weber: Essays in Sociology.* New York: Oxford University Press, 1946.

Mills, C. Wright. *White Collar: The American Middle Classes.* New York: Oxford University Press, 1951.

Mills, C. Wright. *The Power Elite.* New York: Oxford University Press, 1956.

Murdock, George. "The Cross-cultural Survey." *American Sociological Review* 3 (1940): 361–70.

Murdock, George. "The Common Denominator of Cultures." In *The Science of Man in the World Crisis*, edited by Robert Linton. New York: Columbia University Press, 1945, 123–42.

Murdock, George. *Social Structure*. New York: Macmillan, 1949.

Murdock, George. *Outline of Cultural Materials*. 3rd ed. New Haven: Human Relations Area Files, 1950.

Myrdal, Gunnar, with Richard Sterner and Arnold Rose. *An American Dilemma*. New York: Harper & Row, 1944.

Nisbet, Robert. *The Quest for Community*. New York: Oxford University Press, 1953.

Nisbet, Robert. *Emile Durkheim*. Englewood Cliffs, N.J.: Prentice-Hall, 1965.

Nisbet, Robert. *The Social Bond*. New York: Alfred Knopf, 1970.

Nisbet, Robert. *Sociology as an Art Form*. New York: Oxford University Press, 1976.

Ogburn, William. *Social Change*. New York: Viking Press, 1922.

Ogburn, William. *The Social Effects of Aviation*. Boston: Houghton Mifflin, 1946.

Ogburn, William. "The Wolf Boy of Agra." *American Journal of Sociology* 64 (1959): 499–554.

Pareto, Vilfredo. *The Treatise in General Sociology*. Reprinted in part in *The Mind and Society*, edited by Arthur Livingston. New York: Dover, 1963.

Park, Robert, and Ernest W. Burgess. *Introduction to the Science of Sociology*. Chicago: University of Chicago Press, 1921.

Park, Robert, and H. A. Miller. *Old World Traits Transplanted*. New York: Harper & Brothers, 1921.

Park, Robert; Ernest W. Burgess; and R. D. McKenzie. *The City*. Chicago: University of Chicago Press, 1925.

Park, Robert. *Race and Culture*. Glencoe, Ill.: Free Press, 1949.

Parsons, Talcott. *The Structure of Social Action*. New York: Free Press, 1937.

Parsons, Talcott. *The Social System*. New York: Free Press, 1951.

Parsons, Talcott. *Essays in Sociological Theory*. New York: Free Press, 1954.

Parsons, Talcott. *Family, Socialization, and Interaction Process*. New York: Free Press, 1955.

Parsons, Talcott. *Structure and Process in Modern Society*. New York: Free Press, 1960.

Parsons, Talcott; Edward Shils; Kaspar Naegle; and Jesse R. Pitts, eds. *Theories of Society*. New York: Free Press, 1961.

Parsons, Talcott. *Societies: Evolutionary and Comparative Perspectives*. Englewood Cliffs, N.J.: Prentice-Hall, 1966.

Redfield, Robert. *Tepoztlan: A Mexican Village.* Chicago: University of Chicago Press, 1930.

Redfield, Robert. *The Folk Culture of Yucatán.* Chicago: University of Chicago Press. 1941.

Redfield, Robert. *The Primitive World and Its Transformations.* Ithaca: Cornell, 1953.

Redfield, Robert. *Chan Kom, a Maya Village.* Chicago: University of Chicago Press, 1964.

Redfield, Robert. *A Village That Chose Progress.* Chicago: University of Chicago Press, 1964.

Redfield, Robert. *The Little Community, Peasant Society and Culture.* Chicago: University of Chicago Press, 1965.

Riesman, David. *Constraint and Variety in American Education.* Garden City, N.Y.: Doubleday, Anchor, 1958.

Riesman, David. *The Lonely Crowd.* New Haven: Yale University Press, 1969.

Simmel, Georg. *The Sociology of Georg Simmel.* Translated by Kurt Wolff. New York: Free Press, 1950.

Simmel, Georg. *Conflict.* Translated by Reinhard Bendix. Glencoe, Ill.: Free Press, 1955.

Simmel, Georg. "The Significance of Numbers for Social Life." In *Small Groups,* rev. ed., edited by A. Paul Hare, Edgar Borgatta, and Robert Bales. New York: Alfred Knopf, 1965.

Smelser, Neil J., and Seymour M. Lipset, eds. *Social Structure and Mobility in Economic Development,* Chicago: Aldine, 1966.

Sorokin, Pitirim A. *Contemporary Sociological Theories.* New York: Harper & Row, 1928.

Sorokin, Pitirim A. *Social and Cultural Dynamics.* New York: American Book Co., 1941.

Sorokin, Pitirim A. *Society, Culture, and Personality.* New York: Harper & Row, 1947.

Sorokin, Pitirim A. *The Revolution of Humanity.* Boston: Beacon Press, 1948.

Sorokin, Pitirim A. *Fads and Foibles in Modern Sociology and Related Sciences.* Chicago: Regnery, 1956.

Sorokin, Pitirim A., and Carle C. Zimmerman. *Principles of Rural-Urban Sociology.* New York: Holt, Reinhart & Winston, 1929.

Spencer, Herbert. *Social Statics.* London: Appleton, 1865.

Spencer, Herbert. *Descriptive Sociology.* 8 vols. London: Williams & Norgate, 1873-1885.

Spencer, Herbert. *The Study of Sociology.* London: Appleton, 1874.

Sumner, William Graham. *Folkways.* Boston: Ginn, 1907.

Sumner, William Graham and Albert G. Keller. *The Science of Society.* 4 vol. New Haven: Yale University Press, 1927–28.

Sumner, William Graham. *Essays.* Edited by Albert G. Keller and Maurice Davie. 2 vols. New Haven: Yale University Press, 1934.

Sutherland, Edwin H. "White Collar Criminality." *American Sociological Review* 5 (1940): 1–12.

Sutherland, Edwin H. "Is White Collar Crime, Crime?" *American Sociological Review* 10 (1945): 132–139.

Sutherland, Edwin H. *White Collar Crime.* New York: Dryden, 1949.

Sutherland, Edwin H., and Donald R. Cressey. *Criminology.* 8th ed. Philadelphia: Lippincott, 1970.

Szasz, Thomas. *The Myth of Mental Illness: Foundations of a Theory of Personal Conduct.* New York: Harper & Row, 1961.

Szasz, Thomas. *Psychiatric Justice.* New York: Macmillan, 1965.

Szasz, Thomas. *The Manufacture of Madness.* New York: Harper & Row, 1970.

Thomas, William I., and Florian Znaniecki. *The Polish Peasant in Europe and America.* 5 vols. Chicago: University of Chicago Press, 1918-1920.

Thomas, William I. *The Unadjusted Girl.* Boston: Little, Brown, 1923.

Thomas, William I. *The Child in America.* New York: Alfred Knopf, 1928.

Thomas, William I. *Social Behavior and Personality.* Edited by Edmund H. Volkart. New York: Social Science Research Council, 1951.

Toennies, Ferdinand. *Fundamental Concepts of Sociology* (Gemeinschaft und Gesellschaft). Translated by C. P. Loomis. New York: American Book Co., 1940.

Veblen, Thorstein. *The Theory of the Leisure Class.* New York: Macmillan, 1899.

Veblen, Thorstein. *The Higher Learning in America.* New York: Huebsch, 1918.

Warner, W. Lloyd. "Murngin Warfare." *Oceania* 1 (1931): 457–494.

Warner, W. Lloyd, and Paul S. Lunt. *The Social Life of a Modern Community.* New Haven: Yale University Press, 1941.

Warner, W. Lloyd. *The Social Status of a Modern Community.* New Haven: Yale University Press, 1942.

Warner, W. Lloyd, and J. O. Low. *The Social System of a Modern Factory.* New Haven: Yale University Press, 1947.

Warner, W. Lloyd; Machia Meeker; and Kenneth Eills. *Social Class in America.* Gloucester, Mass.: P. Smith, 1957.

Weber, Max. *The Protestant Ethic and the Spirit of Capitalism.* Trans. by T. Parsons. London: Allen & Unwin, 1930.

Weber, Max. *The Theory of Social and Economic Organization.* Trans. by A. M. Henderson and T. Parsons. New York: Oxford University Press, 1947.

Weber, Max. *The Religion of China: Confucianism and Taoism.* Trans. by H. H. Gerth. Glencoe, Ill.: Free Press, 1951.

Weber, Max. *The City.* Trans. by G. Neuwirth and D. Martindale. Glencoe, Ill.: Free Press, 1958.

Whyte, William F. *Human Relations in the Restaurant Industry.* New York: McGraw-Hill, 1948.

Whyte, William F. *Patterns for Industrial Peace.* New York: Harper & Row, 1951.

Whyte, William F. *Street Corner Society.* Chicago: University of Chicago Press, 1955.

Whyte, William F. *Men at Work.* Homewood, Ill.: Dorsey, 1961.

Whyte, William F. *Man and Organization.* Homewood, Ill.: Irwin, 1959.

Williams, Robin M. *Strangers Next Door.* Englewood Cliffs, N.J.: Prentice-Hall, 1964.

Williams, Robin M. *American Society.* New York: Alfred Knopf, 1970.

Wirth, Louis. *The Ghetto.* Chicago: University of Chicago Press, 1928.

Wirth, Louis. "Urbanism as a Way of Life," *American Journal of Sociology* 44 (1938): 3–24.

Znaniecki, Florian. *The Social Role of the Man of Knowledge.* New York: Columbia University Press, 1940.

Index

Academic Mind(Lazarsfeld), 170
"Academic Procession"(Riesman), 185
Active Society(Etzioni), 159
Adam Smith and Modern Sociology (Small), 64
Adler, Alfred, 124
Adolescent Society(Coleman), 154
Aging in Western Societies (Burgess), 77
Allport, Gordon, 111-13
America, early sociological work in, 49-70
American Association for the Abolition of Involuntary Mental Hospitalization, 141
American Association of University Professors, 117
American Indians, 114
American Journal of Sociology, 62, 85, 106
American Life(Warner), 104
American Society: A Sociological Interpretation(Williams), 186
American Sociological Society, 41, 62, 73
American Sociology, 75
An American Dilemma(Myrdal), 137-38
Anomie, 18, 174-76
Anthropology, 113-16, 129-34, 138-40
Arbitrary will, 36-38
Argonauts of the Western Pacific (Malinowski), 131
Assimilation, 61, 104-5
Association Polytechnique, 8

Asylums: Essays on the Social Situation of Mental Patients and Other Inmates(Goffman), 164

Bagehot, Walter, 14
Baldwin, James, 50
Barbarism, modern, 2
Becker, Howard S., 146-47
Bell, Daniel, 147-49
Bendix, Reinhard, 71, 73-75, 172
Benedict, Ruth, 111, 114-17, 142
Berger, Peter, 150-51
Bernard, Claude, 12
Blau, Peter M., 151-53
Blumer, Herbert, 58, 163
Boas, Franz, 113, 114, 132
Boston, 105, 162-63
Boys in White(Hughes), 85
Breuer, Josef, 121
Brücke, Ernst von, 119
Buecher, Karl, 129
Bureaucracy, 44-46, 151, 165
Bureau of Applied Social Research (Columbia University), 170, 174
Burgess, Ernest W., 61, 71, 75-77

Calvinism, 42-44
Canadian Sociological and Anthropological Society, 85
Can Science Save Us?(Lundberg), 87
Capitalism, 42
Caplow, Theodore, 160
Carey, Henry C., 19
Castle, Helen, 56
Chan Kom, a Mayan Village (Redfield), 140
Chapin, F. Stuart, 70, 72, 77-79

Character and Social Structure
  (Gerth and Mills), 93
Charcot, Jean Martin, 119
Cheyenne Indians, 116
Child in America(Thomas), 67
China, 25
Chrysanthemum and the Sword
  (Benedict), 116
Circulation of elites(Pareto), 28
City life, 106-8
*Class and Class Conflict in Industrial
  Society*(Dahrendorf), 157
Class struggle(Marx), 24-25, 66
Colby College(Maine), 62
Coleman, James S., 153-54
Collective conscience(Durkheim),
  16
Coming Crisis of Western Sociology
  (Gouldner), 165
Coming of Age in Samoa(Mead),
  132
Coming of Post-Industrial Society
  (Bell), 149
Communist Manifesto(Marx and
  Engels), 23
Communist revolution, 25
Community and Power(Nisbet), 177
*Comparative Analysis of Complex
  Organizations*(Etzioni), 160
Compliance relationship (Etzioni),
  160
Comte, Auguste, 1-2, 3, 7, 8-12, 29,
  31, 32, 39, 62
"Concept of the Guardian Spirit in
  North America"(Benedict), 114
Condorcet, Marie Jean Antoine
  Nicholas de Caritat, 10
Conflict, social, 31
Conflict(Simmel), 75
Conspicuous consumption(Veblen),
  142
*Constraint and Variety in American
  Education*(Riesman), 185
Contemporary American Institutions
  (Chapin), 77
Contemporary Sociological Theory
  (Sorokin), 101
Cooley, Charles Horton, 49, 50-53,
  56, 58, 110
*Cooperation and Conflict Among
  Primitive Peoples*(Mead), 132

Coral Gardens and Their Magic
  (Malinowski), 131
Coser, Lewis A., 26, 32, 154-55
Cosmopolitans/locals(Gouldner),
  165
Cournot, Antoine Augustin, 34
Cours de philosophie positive
  (Comte), 10
Cressey, Donald G., 101, 155-57
Criminal behavior, 125
Criminology, 101-3, 155-57
Cultural change, 132
Culture and community, 88-90
Cultural imperatives(Malinowski),
  . 131
Cultural lag(Ogburn), 97
*Cultural Patterns and Technological
  Change*(Mead), 132
Cultural Transformation(Mead),
  132
Culture, sociology of, 98-101,
  114-16
Current Sociology, 73

Dahrendorf, Ralf, 25, 26, 157-59
Darwin, Charles, 7, 12-14, 21, 32
Das Kapital(Marx), 24
Davis, Kingsley, 72, 79-82
Definition of the situation(Thomas),
  68
Democracy and Education(Dewey),
  117
Department of Social Relations
  (Harvard), 179
Descent of Man(Darwin), 14
Deviant behavior, 101-3, 146
Dewey, John, 56, 58, 111, 116-19
Differential association
  (Sutherland), 101-3, 155
"Dilemmas and Contradiction of
  Status"(Hughes), 85
Division of Labor in Society
  (Durkheim), 16
Dobu people of Melanesia, 114
Duhem, Pierre, 12
Durkheim, Emile, 7, 8, 14-19, 32,
  36, 52, 55, 113, 117, 138, 179
Dynamic Sociology(Ward), 39
Dynamics of Bureaucracy(Blau),
  151

Economic and Philosophical Manuscripts(Marx), 24
Economics, 24, 26
Economist, 32
Education, 117-19, 153-54 185, sociology of, 84
Ego and the Id(Freud), 122
Elementary Forms of Religious Life (Durkheim), 17
Elites, 28-29, 90, 93-95
Elmtown's Youth(Hollingshead), 84
Engels, Friedrich, 22
Equality of Educational Opportunity (Coleman), 153
Essential will, 36-38
Ethnic groups, 104-5
Ethnocentrism(Sumner), 66
Ethnology, 138, 140, 163
Etzioni, Amitai W., 159-62
Evolution, 39, 55
Exchange and Power in Social Life (Blau), 153
Experience and Education(Dewey), 117
Experimental Sociology (Greenwood), 79

Faces in the Crowd(Riesman), 183
Factory Act of 1833(Britain), 22
Fads and Foibles in Modern Sociology and Related Sciences (Sorokin), 101
Family, 168, structure, 82-83
Family, The(Goode), 83
Faris, Ellsworth, 58
Field theory(Lewin), 127
First New Nation(Lipset), 174
Folk Culture of Yucatan(Redfield), 138
Folkways(Sumner), 66
Foundations of Sociology (Lundberg), 87
Four wishes of man(Thomas), 70
Fraser, James G., 129
French Canada in Transition (Hughes), 85
Freud, Sigmund, 52, 58, 93, 111, 119-24, 125, 179
From Instinct to Character (Fromm), 127
Fromm, Erich, 111, 124-27

From Max Weber(Gerth and Mills), 93
Functional anthropology (Malinowski), 131
Functions of Social Conflict(Coser), 32, 154-55

Gans, Herbert, 162-63, 168
Gatekeeper(Lewin), 129
Geer, Blanche, 146
Gemeinschaft und Gesellschaft (Toennies), 36-38
General Sociology(Small), 62
Genetic Fix(Etzioni), 159
Germany, 29
Gerth, Hans, 93
Ghetto(Wirth), 106
Gibbs, William, 28
Giddings, Franklin, 36, 49, 50, 53-56, 77, 95
Goffman, Erving, 103, 163-64
Golden Bough(Fraser), 129
Goode, William, 71, 82-83
Gouldner, Alvin W., 164-66
Greenwood, Ernest, 79
Grote, George, 8
Group dynamics movement, 127
Groups, 166-68
Guardian spirit complex(Benedict), 114
Gumplowicz, Ludwig, 14

Higher Learning in America (Veblen), 144
Hollingshead, August B., 71, 72, 84-85
Homans, George C., 26, 166-68
Homeless Mind(Berger), 150
Hughes, Everett, 71, 85-87
Human association, process of (Small), 62
Human ecology(Park & Burgess), 61, 75-77
Human Group(Homans), 166
Humanistic coefficient(Znaniecki), 108-10
Human Nature and the Social Order (Cooley), 50
Human Relations Area Files, 135
Human Society(Davis), 80
Hungary, 90

Ideal types(Weber), 46-47
Ideas, role of, 41
Ideology and Utopia(Mannheim), 92
Images of Man(Mills), 93
Impression management(Goffman), 164
Industrialism, 22-26
Industrial Revolution, 22, 25
Inner-directed/other-directed societies(Riesman), 183-85
Institutions, 165
Intellectual elite, 90-92
Interests, theory of(Small), 62
Interpretation of Dreams(Freud), 121, 122
Introduction to the Science of Sociology(Park & Burgess), 32, 61, 75
Invention, social effects of, 97-98
Invitation to Sociology(Berger), 150
Iron law of oligarchy(Michels), 134, 171, 172

James, William, 50, 56
Japanese culture, 116
Jews, identity problem of, 129

Kant, Immanuel, 29, 31
Kassowitz, Children's Clinic (Vienna), 121
Keller, Albert G., 66
Kennedy, John F., quoted, 2
Knowledge for What?(Lund), 89
Komarovsky, Mirra, 168-70
Kornhauser, William, 29

Labeling theory, 147
Lagrange, Joseph L., 11
Language, 58
Laplace, Pierre Simon de, 11
Latent and manifest function (Merton), 176
Latent Structure Analysis (Lazarsfeld), 170
Law of the aggregation of matter (Ward), 39
Law of the three states(Comte), 39
Laws of Inflation(Tarde), 34
Lazarsfeld, Paul F., 170-71, 174, 186

Levittowners(Gans), 162-63
Lewin, Kurt, 111, 127-29
Lipset, Seymour M., 73, 171-74
Listen Yankee(Mills), 93
Lobhouse, L. T., 129
Lombroso, Cesare, 101
London School of Economics, 131
Lonely Crowd(Riesman), 183
Looking-glass self(Cooley), 52
Lundberg, George, 72, 87-88
Lynd, Helen, 88
Lynd, Robert S., 71, 72, 88-90, 168

Mach, Ernst, 12
MacIver, award, 73, 83
Male and Female(Mead), 132
Malinowski, Bronislaw, 111, 129-31
Malthus, Thomas, 7, 19-21
Managerial classes, 95
Mannheim, Karl, 71, 90-92, 150
Manufacture of Madness(Szasz), 142
Marginal man, 61
Marijuana studies, 146-47
Marshall, Alfred, 179
Marx, Karl, 7, 8, 22-26, 38, 41, 64, 66, 125, 159
Marxists, The(Mills), 93
Mass communications, 170
Mayo-Smith, Richmond, 56
Mead, George Herbert, 49, 50, 52, 56-59, 93, 147, 151
Mead, Margaret, 111, 116, 132-34
Meaning of the Social Sciences (Small), 64
Mechanical solidarity(Durkheim), 16
Mental health/illness, 84-85, 141-42
Merton, Robert, 18, 26, 174-77
Michels, Robert, 111, 134-35, 171, 172
Middletown(Lynd and Lynd), 88
Middletown in Transition(Lynd and Lynd), 88
Mill, John Stuart, 8, 12
Mills, C. Wright, 28, 72, 93-95, 171
Mind, Self and Society(Mead), 58
Mind and Society(ed., Livingston), 26
Minorities, 108
Modern Organizations(Etzioni), 160

"Modern Society"(Bendix), 75
Money, 29-31
Moore, Wilbert, 72, 80-82
Muncie, Indiana, 88
Murdock, George P., 111, 135
Myrdal, Gunnar, 111, 135, 137-38
Myth of Mental Illness(Szasz), 141

Nature of Prejudice(Allport), 112
Nazism, 113
New England, 104
New Lives for Old(Mead), 132
New Men of Power(Mills), 93
Nietzsche, Friedrich, 114
Nisbet, Robert A., 177-79

Oedipus complex(Freud), 123-24
Ogburn, William, 71, 77, 95-98, 144
Oligarchy, 134, 172
Operationalism, 88
Organic solidarity(Durkheim), 16
Organization theory, 160
Origin of Species(Darwin), 12, 32
Other People's Money(Cressey), 157
Other Side, The(Becker), 147
Outsiders(Becker), 147

Palauans of Micronesia, 132
Pareto, Vilfredo, 7, 8, 26-29, 179
Park, Robert Ezra, 49, 50, 59-61, 75, 103, 106
Parsons, Talcott, 26, 29, 56, 66, 80, 101, 160, 166, 179-83
Patterns of Culture(Benedict), 114 142
Patterns of Industrial Bureaucracy (Gouldner), 165
Pattern variables(Parsons), 182
Peasant Society and Culture (Redfield), 140
People's Choice(Lazarsfeld), 170
Personal Influence(Lazarsfeld), 170
Personality development, 58-59
Personality types, three(Thomas), 70
Philosophy of Money(Simmel), 29-31
Polish Peasant in Europe and America(Thomas & Znaniecki), 67, 68, 108

Political institutions, 171-72
Political Man(Lipset), 171
Political Parties(Michels), 134
"Political Sociology"(Bendix and Lipset), 73
Population theory(Malthus), 19-21
Postman, Allan, 112
Power/involvement classification, 160, 162
Power Elite(Mills), 93
Power elite thesis(Mills), 95
Prejudice, 112-13
Principle of consciousness of kind (Giddings), 55
Principles of Criminology (Sutherland and Cressey), 101, 155
Principles of Sociology (Giddings), 53
Principles of Sociology (Spencer), 34
Progress, 39-41
Progressive education(Dewey), 117
Protestant Ethic(Weber), 41, 42
Psychiatric Justice(Szasz), 142
Psychiatry/psychology, 121-24 141-42
Pyramids of Sacrifice: Political Ethics and Social Change (Berger), 150

Quest for Community(Nisbet), 177

Race relations, 137
Radcliffe-Brown, A. R., 131, 138
Radio Research(Lazarsfeld), 170
Rank, Otto, 124
Rank order of discrimination (Myrdal), 137
Rationality theory(Weber), 44
Ratzenhofer, Gustav, 14, 62
Redfield, Robert, 111, 138-41
Redlich, E. C., 84
Religion, sociology of, 17-18, 150
Research Center for Group Dynamics(MIT), 127
Riesman, David, 183-85
Role-set(Merton), 174, 176
Ross, E. A., 36
Rules of the Sociological Method (Durkheim), 17

Rumor, 112-13
Russia, 25

"Sadler Report" to Parliament, 22
Saint-Simon, Claude Henri de
    Rouvroy, 8, 10
School and Society(Dewey), 117
Science, study of, 87
Science of Society(Sumner and
    Keller), 66
Sciences, hierarchy of, 10-11
Scott, Richard, 151
Self-fulfilling prophecy(Thomas),
    68, 70
Seligman, C. G., 129
Sex roles, 168
Sexual Life of Savages
    (Malinowski), 131
*Sexual Temperament in Three
    Primitive Societies*(Mead), 132
Simmel, Georg, 7, 8, 29-32, 75, 155
Small, Albion, 49, 50, 61-64
Smith, Adam, 19, 21, 55
Smith, T. V., 58
Social and Cultural Dynamics
    (Sorokin), 98, 100
*Social Behavior: Its Elementary
    Forms*(Homans), 166
Social Behavior and Personality
    (ed., Volkart), 67
Social Bond (Nisbet), 178
Social Change(Chapin), 79
Social Change(Ogburn), 97
Social Class and Mental Illness
    (Hollingshead and Redlich), 84
Social Construction of Reality
    (Berger), 150
Social Darwinism, 14, 49, 55, 66
Social dynamics, 55-56
Social Effects of Aviation
    (Ogburn), 95
Social evolution(Spencer), 32
Social facts(Durkheim), 17
Social groups, organization of,
    36-38
Social institutions, 77-79
Social integration(Durkheim),
    14, 16
Social inventions, 2
Social kinetics(Giddings), 55
Social Laws(Tarde), 34

Social Logic(Tarde), 34
*Social Mobility in Industrial
    Society*(Lipset and Bendix),
    73, 104
Social norms, 38-39
Social order/integration, 104
Social Organization(Cooley), 50
Social Problems, 146
Social Process(Cooley), 50
Social psychology, 111-12, 124-25,
    127
Social Research(Lundberg), 88
Social space(Lewin), 127
Social statics(Giddings), 55
Social Statics(Spencer), 34
Social stratification(Davis and
    Moore), 80-82, 84-85
Social Structure(Murdock), 135
Social System(Parsons), 182
*Social System of the Modern
    Factory*(Warner), 105
*Social Systems of American Ethnic
    Groups*(Warner), 104-5
Social Theory and Social Structure
    (Merton), 18, 176
Société positiviste, 10
Society, Culture and Personality
    (Sorokin), 101
*Sociological Eye: Selected Papers
    on Work, Self, and the Study of
    Society*(Hughes), 85
Sociological Imagination(Mills), 93
Sociological Theories of Today
    (Sorokin), 101
Sociology: American beginnings,
    49-70; contributions of
    nonsociologists, 111-45, defined,
    3-4; methodological
    breakthroughs, 71-110; origins of,
    1-2, 7-47; present perspectives,
    145-88; of religion, 17-18, 150;
    urban, 59-61; work, 73-75, 85-87,
    93-95
Sociology as an Art Form(Nisbet),
    178
Sociology of Georg Simmel
    (Wolff), 32
"Sociology of the family"
    (Goode), 83
Sociology of religion, 17-18, 151
Sociology Today, 83

Sorokin, Pitirim, 72, 98-101, 110
Source Book of Social Origins
  (Thomas), 67
Soziologie(Simmel), 31
Spencer, Herbert, 7, 12, 29, 31,
  32-34, 39, 52, 53, 56, 64, 93
Status inconsistency(Hughes), 87
Status panic(Mills), 93
Strangers Next Door(Williams),
  188
Street Corner Society(Whyte),
  72, 105, 168
Structural functionalism, 17, 80-82
Structure of Social Action
  (Parsons), 179
Studies in Hysteria(Freud), 121
Studies in Leadership(Gouldner),
  165
Study of Sociology(Spencer), 34
Suchman, Edward, 186
Suicide, 18-19
Sumner, William Graham, 14, 39,
  49, 64-67
Superego(Freud), 122-23
Sutherland, Edwin H., 72, 101-3
Synergy(Ward), 39
Szasz, Thomas, 111, 141-42

Tarde, Gabriel, 7, 8, 34-36, 39
Technology and social change,
  142, 144
Tepoztlan: A Mexican Village
  (Redfield), 138
Theft of the Nation(Cressey), 157
Theory of imitation(Tarde), 34-36
Theory of the Leisure Class
  (Veblen), 142
Thomas, William I., 49, 50, 56, 58,
  67-70, 87, 108, 176
Thomas theorem, 68
*Three Essays on the Theory of
  Sexuality*(Freud), 121
Toennies, Ferdinand, 7, 36-39, 178
Toleration, 55
Total institution(Goffman), 164
Totem and Taboo(Freud), 123
Trans Action Magazine, 164
Treatise on General Sociology
  (Pareto), 26
Trobriand Islanders, 131

Unadjusted Girl(Thomas),
  67, 68, 70
Unemployed Man and His Family
  (Komarovsky), 168
Union Democracy(Lipset, Trow
  and Coleman), 134, 172
Universal Opposition(Tarde), 34
Universals, search for, 180
University of Chicago: department
  of sociology, 50, 56, 59, 62, 67,
  75, 106, 108; laboratory school,
  117
University of Minnesota, 77
University of Vienna, 119
"Urbanism as a Way of Life"
  (Wirth), 106
Urban sociology, 59-61
Urban Villagers(Gans), 162-63, 168

Veblen, Thorstein, 97, 111, 142-44
Verifiability doctrine, 11
Village That Chose Progress
  (Redfield), 140
Volkart, Edmund H., 67
Voting(Lazarsfeld), 170

Ward, Lester Frank, 7, 39-41, 50,
  53, 56, 62, 64
Warner, William Lloyd, 61, 71, 72,
  103-5
Washington, Booker T., 59
Washington University, 87
Wealth of Nations(Smith), 19, 64
Weber, Max, 7, 8, 41-47, 93,
  160
Westermarck, Edward A., 129
*White Collar: The American Middle
  Class*(Mills), 93
Whyte, William F., 71, 72,
  105-6, 168
Wildcat Strike(Gouldner), 165
Will, analysis of, 36
Williams, Robin M., 186-88
Wirth, Louis, 75, 106-8
Wolff, Kurt, 32
Women in the Modern World
  (Komarovsky), 168
Work, sociology of, 73-75,
  85-87, 93-95
Work and Authority in Industry
  (Bendix), 73, 75

*World Revolution and Family
  Patterns*(Goode), 82
Wundt, William, 129

Yale Cross Cultural Survey, 135
Yankee City series(Warner),
  72, 103-4

Yucatan Peninsula, 138

Znaniecki, Florian, 67, 68, 72,
  108-10
Zuni of New Mexico, 114
Zweckrationell action(Weber), 44